GOOD NEWS IN EXILE

Good News in Exile

Three Pastors Offer a
Hopeful Vision for the Church

Martin B. Copenhaver
Anthony B. Robinson
William H. Willimon

WILLIAM B. EERDMANS PUBLISHING COMPANY
GRAND RAPIDS, MICHIGAN / CAMBRIDGE, U.K.

© 1999 Wm. B. Eerdmans Publishing Co.
255 Jefferson Ave. S.E., Grand Rapids, Michigan 49503 /
P.O. Box 163, Cambridge CB3 9PU U.K.

Printed in the United States of America

04 03 02 01 00 99   7 6 5 4 3 2 1

Library of Congress Cataloging-in-Publication Data

Copenhaver, Martin B., 1954-
Good news in exile: three pastors offer a hopeful vision for the church /
Martin B. Copenhaver, Anthony B. Robinson, William H. Willimon.
p.   cm.
ISBN 0-8028-4604-1 (pbk.: alk. paper)
1. Theology, Practical.   2. Protestant churches—United States.
I. Robinson, Anthony B.   II. Willimon, William H.   III. Title.
BV3.C66   1999
253—dc21   98-49667
                                                  CIP

This book is dedicated to:

Wellesley Congregational Church,
United Church of Christ

Plymouth Congregational Church,
United Church of Christ

Duke University Chapel

and the other congregations
we have been privileged to serve.

Contents

Foreword   ix
Walter Brueggemann

Introduction   1

Autobiographical Prefaces

Growing Up Liberal and Beyond   5
Martin B. Copenhaver

The Making of a Post-Liberal   13
Anthony B. Robinson

Up from Liberalism   27
William H. Willimon

Scripture: Our Home in Exile   33

Preaching and Speech: Words Make Worlds   45

Ritual and Sacrament: Beyond Words   59

Christian Formation and the Teaching Ministry:
Becoming Christian   75

Mission and Social Action: Beyond Common Sense   91

Conversion: New Creation   107

Foreword

It is said that it is amazing to see a dog play checkers, even if the dog does not win, because it is an odd and unnatural act. In some circles, given the diminishment of ministry, it is thought as odd to see pastors doing theology as it is to see a dog playing checkers. These three first-rate pastors, against such a parallelism between checkers and theology, make clear that doing serious pastoral theology is neither odd nor unnatural, even if it has become rare among us. It is rather one of the most normal, appropriate, and needed acts of pastoral ministry, for critical theological reflection is urgent and welcome in church traditions that have nearly lost their way.

This book by these three remarkable colleagues (who represent quite different and distinct theological backgrounds) is a welcome contribution to the current ferment in church life. Of course this offer of practical theology does not begin *de novo,* for they have read and thought seriously about the interpretive offerings of George Lindbeck and Stanley Hauerwas. They have understood that the old "liberal," mainline churches are now deprivileged and sidelined and are in a new situation that requires different perspectives, different categories, and different interpretations. This "post-liberal" posture, however, should not for an instant be understood as any concession to old-line conservatism, for that is not what they intend. Indeed, they see clearly that old-line liberalism and old-line conservatism are two peas in a pod, and neither will avail much now. Their work is rather a recognition that the old-line "liberal" churches are now without privilege, advantage, or clout, and so find themselves in something of an "exile," that is, in a context of doing faith in an environment that is variously hostile or indifferent to that faith. Such a new context may turn out to be hugely emancipatory for the church.

I am encouraged that these three pastor-theologians are not in any direct way "church politicians" who vie for impact in organizational enterprises. They are not trying to impose. Gratefully they are not one more voice announcing that they occupy the "middle ground," for it does seem that every contentious caucus in the church offers itself as the "happy center."

Rather than making such a characteristically self-serving claim, these three understand that the deprivileged church now faces an invitation to a peculiar identity so that it can travel light, because it does not need to be a "cultural carrier" for all things good and noble. Insisting that now "it is all conversion," the book suggests that the United States is a mission field in which all sorts of would-be believers still wait to be invited to the peculiar missional identity of the Christian.

Not everything here is new, for much of the book reflects what is now standard fare in such discussions. What is new is that here speak pastoral voices considering how this new challenge of the gospel takes shape in the actual practice of congregational life.

— The book teems with concrete pastoral examples that show how new interpretive categories work "on the ground."
— The book pays attention to the discipline of the lectionary. While the lectionary is of course open to criticism, it does deliver the church from "Lone Ranger ministry" and hints of ecclesial and integral dimensions of the pastoral office.
— The book is acutely sensitive to sacramental matters that count for a great deal with exiles. When the congregation cannot any longer depend upon mechanical cultural supports, it must fall back on its own peculiar indices of the holy that make life livable.
— The book hints at openness to the traditions of Pentecostalism

as an alternative to old-line liberal rationality, an awareness that God's purpose and power do not necessarily inhabit social respectability and control.

— The book underscores the teaching function of the ministry, an accent on the central claims of faith that override the emotive quality of "therapeutic" models of ministry.

One can see why the authors conclude that "the natural habitat of theology is the church." The book is a powerful summons and invitation to focus upon the congregation as the primary unit for the church. That will require, in many places, a serious reappropriation of the pastoral office and an ecclesiology that goes back to missional categories. Thanks is due to Martin, Tony, and Will for their courage in making such an insistence.

In the context of checkers, one can occasionally hear the dog say to the playing partner, "Your move." In this powerful work of pastoral theology toward new missional identity, one can hear these three saying to the church they address, "Your move." They are calling for a move of repentance, passion, and intentionality, a move into the liberty of exile, unencumbered, free for distinctiveness that eschews any pet project — liberal or conservative — distinctiveness that is a gift from God before it is mission in the world.

Columbia Theological Seminary   WALTER BRUEGGEMANN
March 26, 1998

Introduction

This book began as a conversation among three friends. It took shape as we swapped stories about our congregations, reflected on our experiences, and talked about our convictions, as pastoral colleagues are wont to do. Through those conversations we discovered that, from quite different starting points, we have come to something that resembles a common destination.

We were raised in three different denominations that used to be referred to as "mainline Protestant." We now serve congregations in two of those denominations: the United Methodist Church and the United Church of Christ. We are from the South, the Northwest, and the Northeast. Currently, we serve as pastors in very different settings: a college campus in the South, the center of a major city on one coast, and a suburb of another city on the other coast.

Yet, out of that diversity of background and setting, we have much in common. We can imagine some of our colleagues responding, "Of course you have a lot in common! You are all white male pastors who were born at one end or the other of the baby boom!" It may be best to come clean about that from the beginning. That is all true.

Nevertheless, there are other points of commonality that run deeper than that. We were all brought up in churches that are often called "liberal." We use the term "liberal" not so much in the political sense — as in the dichotomy between "conservative" and "lib-

1

eral" — but in the philosophical sense. That is, we were nurtured in the assumptions of liberalism: that the individual is the sovereign unit of society; that there are certain universally experienced values inherent in all people everywhere; that there is no truth other than that truth which is self-derived; that it is possible to find some neutral philosophical ground whereby conflicts between points of view can be resolved.

Yet each of us, by our own winding paths, has departed from that way of approaching the world and has ended up somewhere quite different. That is, we have come to question the basic assumptions that governed the churches that nurtured us and that, in many ways, are still evident in the churches we serve.

We know that we are not alone in this. Increasingly there is a sense among those who serve the church that something fundamental has changed. So this is not so much a book about how our minds have changed as it is a book about how the world has changed and about how the church might respond faithfully to those changes.

The changes we see are not easily summarized. The implications spread out in so many different directions that no aspect of the life of the church is unaffected. So, in part, this book is an attempt to identify what has changed in various aspects of the life of the church and to trace the implications. We have tried to "connect the dots," and then to stand back far enough to consider the picture that emerges.

This emerging way of understanding the church is sometimes called "post-liberal," but that, of course, is more of a label than a description. And it is not even a very good label at that, because, although clearly we are surrounded by the vestiges of an old and familiar era, we are entering a quite different era, full of risks and opportunities, that is only now beginning to emerge.

We believe that, in many ways, this new era can be described as a time of exile. For North American Protestants it is a time of loss, of relinquishment, of disestablishment. In short, we no longer live under the illusion that we are in charge. That would be "bad news" for us if we did not remember that our God already has considerable experience in working powerfully among those who are in exile. As the history of Israel demonstrates, a time of exile can be particularly rich and fertile. There is opportunity in relinquishment. When we let go of an old reality we have the chance to welcome a new reality in ways we could not have foreseen. The Good News is that now this new world is breaking in among us.

Again, we know that we are not the only ones who have observed this. We write, however, from a particular perspective, grounded in the realities of the parishes we serve. As pastors, we have seen the ways in which these changes touch down in individual lives and in the lives of our congregations. That is the perspective we aim to share in this book.

We begin with three autobiographical prefaces. In each of these accounts we speak individually about where we started and how we ended up where we have. Then, in each of the succeeding chapters, we consider a particular aspect of the church's life, tracing what we see as some of the changes that are evident in our congregations and the particular opportunities that accompany those changes. The areas we address are illustrative of changes that we are sure could be traced in other areas as well. That is, they are intended to be illustrative rather than exhaustive.

As this book began in a conversation, it is written in the hope that the conversation might broaden to include others who love the church, and worry about the church, and yet live with hope. That hope is forged on hard realities, including the loss of much that the church has held dear. If ever there was a time for us to hold fast to a resurrection faith, this is it. And that is Good News, indeed.

Growing Up Liberal and Beyond

MARTIN B. COPENHAVER

Sitting on the four corners of the central intersection in the small suburban town in which I grew up there is the public school, the library, the town hall, and my home church. Every morning an American flag is raised over the lawn in front of each of the four buildings. The church, however, sits on a hill above the other public buildings, as if presiding over all. The church is built of stone, its sturdy Norman architecture seemingly rising out of the massive rock formations that jut forth from the earth throughout the town, as if the stone of the church were rooted in the very foundation of the earth. To this day, when I sing the hymn "The Church's One Foundation" or hear reference to Simon as "the Rock" on which Jesus will build his church, I think of that building.

My father was the senior minister of the church. When he looked out the window of his study, perched high in the church on the hill, he could survey the town as if it were all his parish, and in a sense it was no wonder: during much of the time that my father served there, the church membership was over a third of the population of the town.

Indeed, in ways that everyone took for granted at the time but seem quite remarkable now, when my father was called as pastor to that church he was also called to a privileged position in the wider community. As a Christian minister, his authority was recognized not just in the church but in some way throughout the rest of the town as well. I was once told that, in my hometown, my father's sermons were cited in conversation about current issues almost as often as James Reston's column in *The New York Times*. This is not surprising; in that era both seemed to be working the same beat, holding up different ends of the same civic project, offering trenchant commentary on the events of the day.

Almost as a matter of course, my father would be asked to offer a prayer at the Memorial Day services on the Town Hall lawn or at graduation ceremonies at the public school. Civic organizations customarily would have a seat on the board reserved for a clergyman (they were all men then), and often that seat was occupied by my father. Those who were not members of any church would turn to him for counsel, expecting him to have a compassionate ear and a wise word safe for general consumption (that is, not containing more than trace amounts of religion). Many people outside the congregation would call on him to officiate at their wedding or to have their baby "done" (that is, baptized). In such a setting at such a time, it seemed the natural thing to do.

I did not experience many of the difficulties often associated with growing up as a minister's son. In fact, in both church and town, I delighted in the role. I loved my father, and, as his son, I basked in the overflow of respect in which he was held. I was Little Lord Fauntleroy sliding down the banisters in the palace, the son of royalty given free rein, if not yet the reign of the kingdom. Gratefully, God is continually remixing motives, but I am certain that that was a large part of the appeal of the ministry for me in my early years. I am sure that I imagined that someday I could inherit this kingdom and preside over it in the same way I had seen my father do. But something happened along the way. The church in which I grew up still sits on the same hill today, and I now serve a church that sits on a hill in another town, but today everything has changed. That kingdom does not exist anymore.

Today the world is different from the one into which I was born, and today's church is different from the one in which I was baptized. To a certain extent this could be said in any generation. But many of us sense that what we are experiencing today is something more. It is nothing less than a seismic shift, and, although much of the time American Christians can proceed steadily in the same way we always have, there are times when we can feel the very ground on which we stand tremble.

I was born in 1954, at the epicenter of the baby boom. It was an era in which every respectable, upwardly mobile, and concerned citizen was expected to be in church on Sunday morning and the children were expected to be in Sunday school. The formal photograph of my confirmation class, taken on the front steps of the church, included roughly half my classmates at the school across the street. Many of the rest of my classmates attended the Catholic and Episcopal churches in town. I have since discovered that the year of my birth is inscribed on the cornerstone of countless church school wings across the country.

The year 1954 was the middle of what came to be called both "The American Century" and "The Christian Century." The two were assumed to be inextricably linked. Our nation was experiencing the exhilarating blush of victory in World War II, and there were those who talked with confidence about "winning the world for Christ in this generation."

In 1954, the phrase "under God" was added to the Pledge of Allegiance, and in the same year President Eisenhower made the observation, "Our government makes no sense unless it is founded on a deeply felt religious faith — and I don't care what faith it is." Of course, he said this at a time when "religious faith" was assumed to be synonymous with Christian.

This "kingdom" of American liberal Protestantism no longer exists. We are not in charge anymore, if we ever really were in charge. Many respond to this experience of "exile" by calling for a return to a time when the culture accommodated religious practice and supported the Christian values that we aim to instill in our children, a time when stores were closed on Sundays and prayers were offered in schools on Monday mornings. By contrast, I have come to believe that for liberal Protestants there is no returning to another time and circumstance when we seemed to be charge, and that there are ways in which we can welcome these changes, as un-

7

settling as they may be. That is, I am convinced that there is good news in exile.

I have concluded that our culture's accommodation of Christianity was always rather thin, lulling us into the notion that the world would somehow do our work for us. When the culture at large tipped its hat to religion, we in turn became complacent enough to assume that the job of shaping Christians would be done in the world, rather than in the church. Of course, we should have been suspicious all along. When the gospel that Paul called "a stumbling block to Jews and folly to the Gentiles" becomes widely and easily accepted by the culture at large, something is amiss.

Today the secular culture makes not the slightest apology for defying or simply ignoring the challenges of the gospel. This should not surprise us. The world is once again acting like the world. This leaves the church with the challenge of once again acting like the church. We need to take up the job that was always ours, the job of becoming a community in which Christian lives can be formed. There are great stresses in this time of transition, but there are also unique opportunities. Contrary to Yogi Berra, the future is not like the present, only longer. The future beckons us into a wonderful new world, the outlines of which are only now coming into focus. But it is a vision we can see only if we cease to expect that the future will look just like the past.

I am a child of American liberal Protestantism. Sometimes it seems as if the ways of liberalism are imprinted on my genes, or as if they were in my mother's milk. Indeed, it is telling that my parents met as students in a class taught by Reinhold Niebuhr at Union Theological Seminary. My father's mentor was Harry Emerson Fosdick, who left his indelible stamp on a generation of preachers who came under his tutelage or were inspired by his example.

The preaching I heard growing up revealed an underlying liberal assumption that there is continuity between the best human thought and the Christian gospel (an understanding that is summarized by the title of Nathanael Guptill's 1956 book, *Christianity Does Make Sense,* a typical affirmation of that era). Sermons were generously sprinkled with quotes from virtually every human endeavor. The preacher might use the words of a poet, the findings of a sociologist, the research of a scientist, and the observations of a contemporary journalist to support the sermon's point. To be sure, there were also references to Scripture, but often these references were made as if they were a summary of all that had gone before. The gospel was treated as the capstone of human experience.

There was also talk about Jesus, but the abundance of references to other sources, and the ways in which they were treated as having authority, gave the impression that what we receive from Jesus could be obtained by other means. Often Jesus was used as a kind of crowning sermon illustration, underscoring truths that were there for us to grasp if we were but open to the accumulated wisdom of the ages. How could we not listen to Jesus when other authorities from a variety of disciplines seemed to be saying the same thing in their own ways? An atheist friend once gave this critique of liberal preachers: "You hear what the psychologist says, what the historian says, what *The New York Times* editorial writer says, and then the sermon concludes with, 'And perhaps Jesus said it best . . .'"

Given this background, perhaps it is not surprising that, when I took religion courses in college, initially I was drawn to theologians like Paul Tillich. Tillich had a way of translating the Christian faith into terms that made it sound so reasonable and erudite. Such approaches to the Christian faith reassured me that I could be a Christian and a sophisticated college student at the same time, without giving up anything in the bargain. In those days I interpreted to friends the attraction of going into the ministry by saying, "It is the closest thing in our culture to being a full-time philosopher."

Of course, today I cannot remember that comment without wincing a bit. Now that my motives for being a Christian minister have been thoroughly remixed, that remark stands as a signpost that marks the length of my journey, a journey that reflects changes not only in my own life but also in the church I have been called to serve.

A feminist friend once said to me, with passion and no small hint of exasperation, "If Jesus is just another wise teacher, I have no interest at all. I'll be damned if I'm going to let another *man* tell me

9

how to live my life! If he is not the Son of God, God's Chosen One, the Messiah, then forget about it!" Although her life's story is quite different from mine, her words express well a conviction that, over time, began to overtake me.

That is, I began to ask, "If this Christian story fits in so easily with the culture at large, if it is just a religious form of the common wisdom, if the claims of Christ can be rendered in such a way that they make sense to every thinking person, then why bother?" I would rather go for a walk in the woods (which is just what many in my generation decided to do). What kept me from taking that walk in the woods is that I began to encounter a different gospel. This gospel doesn't "make sense" in any way that the world at large can be expected to recognize. The gospel is more than good advice; it is good news. It has authority, not because of its inherent reasonableness, but because of its source.

I began to discover that the Christian story, for all its familiarity, is perpetually odd. When I was a boy the church seemed like a sturdy pillar of what we used to call "the establishment," like part of the consortium of school, government, and other institutions that all worked together to make us good citizens. Over time I came to see that the church, when it lives up to its charge, is the original counterculture, subverting many of the values that the culture at large holds dear. I came to know a Jesus who doesn't demonstrate the slightest interest in fitting in. He isn't content with offering some helpful observations about life, but instead invites us to receive a new life. He would rather be odd than relevant, and, if we are to follow him, we are to risk being odd ourselves. I found this wonderfully freeing. After all, when we observe the deceit, violence, and greed of our world, why would we want to fit in?

Perhaps most of all, I discovered that the resurrection is not an illustration of anything, but a singular event that is true in a way that reveals that many of our intuitions and experiences are misleading. All the sensible talk and accumulated wisdom of humankind does not prepare us to understand the God that this Jesus reveals. There is a radical discontinuity between the story of this Jesus and what is available to us elsewhere. Instead of concluding, "And perhaps Jesus said it best . . . ," we can only say, "You have heard it said . . . but Jesus says to you . . ."

So, for me, increasingly, the excitement of being a Christian has been in discovering the enduring truth and power in understandings and practices that the liberal church never completely discarded, but at least muted along the way in an effort to fit in with the culture at large. For a liberal (and in many ways I still consider myself one) that can be the most exciting frontier of all. When my contemporaries were experimenting with Transcendental Meditation, I was discovering the ways in which prayer in the name of Jesus can radically alter one's approach to life. When others were feeding their spiritual hunger with mix-and-match New Age beliefs, I found, somewhat to my surprise, that I could feast on the bread that is broken and the cup that is shared at the curious ritual of the Lord's Table. When others were consuming the latest book on "spirituality," I was reading afresh what Karl Barth called "the strange new world of the Bible," and finding in its pages the most exotic spiritual path of all. When others were denouncing the horrors of war by citing the destruction it reaps, the innocent people who were killed, I found myself joining their protests, but on a different basis: I had been called to imitate the ways of one who was willing to die, though he was innocent, rather than seize power through force, whose answer to violence was the cross.

When I began to serve my first church, it was not long before I discovered that I am not qualified to be a full-time philosopher. No congregation I would be willing to serve would be interested in gathering each week to listen to Martin Copenhaver's observations about life. Left on my own, I simply do not have that much to say that is worthwhile. But, gratefully, I could do something else. I could proclaim a story that is more odd, more interesting, and more exciting than anything I could make up. It is a story that I heard first in that church that sits on the hill, albeit in ways that did not reveal to me the full breadth and depth and height of what I have since discovered.

There is an old children's story about a pair of youngsters who happen upon a map that leads to a secret treasure. So they leave home and follow clue after clue, have adventure upon adventure, until the map leads them to the treasure, which is buried in their own back yard where it was all along. And so it has been with me.

We are indeed experiencing a sea-change in the life of the Christian church in our time. The term *sea-change* comes from Shakespeare's *The Tempest,* in which Ariel sings:

"Nothing of him doth fade
But doth suffer a sea-change
Into something rich and strange."

Much of the time it can seem as if the church we love is merely fading away, but those of us who cling to the promise of the Resurrection already know that God has a way of taking the raw stuff of decay and even death and fashioning it into something "rich and strange." This God is not finished yet. And so, I believe, neither is the church.

The Making of a Post-Liberal

ANTHONY B. ROBINSON

In 1991, at the conclusion of my first year at Plymouth Church, a congregation of the United Church of Christ in Seattle, Washington, I preached a sermon on "The State of the Church." I reported on what I had learned in my first twelve months with my new congregation and offered some observations about what I saw as our strengths and needs. I made several recommendations, including the idea that we undertake a long-range planning effort in order to answer the question, What are we trying to accomplish? The idea was well received, and the church council took steps to begin. One of those steps was to engage a consultant, someone with knowledge of larger churches and strategic planning.

A couple of months later our consultant arrived on the scene, unpacked his bags, and began four days of interviewing, observation, and analysis. On the evening of the last day, after having interviewed singly or in groups over a hundred members of the congregation, as well as a smattering of persons from the wider community, the consultant sat down with the twenty-five members of the church council to give a preliminary report.

It all began well enough. The consultant spoke of the congregation's many strengths: its history, location, financial resources, and reputation. Just as members of the council were about to drift off contentedly, he changed direction. "But you have a couple of problems." Then, in a tone as matter-of-fact as if he were giving us an estimate for furnace repairs, he said, "You have a couple of problems. One of them is that you have a Christian in the pulpit. A lot of people are troubled by that." An alert silence was broken by nervous laughter. A nerve had been touched.

I recognize that such a story may be construed as terribly self-serving. I use it with caution. I do not imagine myself as the voice of authentic Christianity in an otherwise lapsed congregation. The consultant's characterization was blunt, too blunt. But it did signal something important. I had come to a different articulation of Christian faith, and a different understanding of the church and the ministry, than the one in which I had been raised in the Congregational, United Church of Christ, and mainline Protestant world. It was different from the understanding of the faith and the church regnant in Plymouth Church in 1990 and in many mainline, liberal Protestant churches.

I want briefly to describe this reigning theology, which I have come to name for myself with the shorthand designation "civic faith." Through the lens of a particular congregation and minister's experience I want to assess the strengths and weaknesses of civic faith and to trace my own evolution from this civic faith to one that might be termed "post-liberal." As cumbersome as that latter designation is, it does serve to say that the choices before us are not adequately described by either the "liberal" or the "conservative" options.

I am a child of thological liberalism and its civic faith expression. As an adult and an ordained minister I have engaged in a lover's quarrel with it. I do not so much seek to retreat from it as to move beyond it. In the concluding part of these observations I will describe what I find my ministry looking like, what excites me, and what kinds of things I find myself aiming to do that I would never have imagined when I went off to seminary in 1973.

"You have a Christian in the pulpit. A lot of people are troubled by that." What did this cryptic statement mean? Can it be an entry point to a larger story?

Seattle's Plymouth Congregational Church could be described as an "old, first church." The modern look of the present church buildings, completed in 1967, belies this description, but the congregation is Seattle's second oldest, preceded only by First Methodist, several blocks away. When a group of Congregationalists gathered in the autumn of 1869 to found a church, the population of the emerging city was only 1,000. Seattle had yet to be officially incorporated. From its earliest years the congregation conceived its mission as one of civilizing this rough-and-tumble city on the nation's westernmost edge. Members of the congregation have served at various times as the city's mayor, as members of the city council, as legislators, and as members of Seattle's school board. At the turn of the century Plymouth members were leaders in the effort to close down Seattle's thriving brothel and gambling establishments. The church also functioned in a role played by many downtown, "first" churches, that of "mother church." Nearly all of Seattle's twenty Congregational churches were spawned, in one way or another, by Plymouth.

Plymouth has a proud history of civic activism. Boys and girls clubs thrived between 1910 and the mid-thirties. Refugee resettlement efforts were undertaken following World War II and the Vietnam War. In the early 1980s the congregation pioneered an innovative low-income housing development program. Today the congregation supports a pioneering ministry to persons experiencing mental illness.

Yet all was not well. The congregation had grown older. In 1990 two-thirds of congregation members were over sixty, a third over eighty years of age. Membership, though relatively stable, was slowly declining. Most Sundays the sanctuary was less than half full. In the late 1980s the congregation found itself paralyzed by an acrimonious conflict regarding divestment of its endowment fund to support the anti-apartheid movement in South Africa. It had become difficult for the congregation to articulate its identity and purpose in a compelling and theological way. Congregational community was fractured by competing interest groups and agendas.

But in some ways these challenges only exposed a much deeper one: the faith and ethos that had animated Plymouth for generations seemed less and less suited to the present and future. Of course, this was not true only of this particular congregation. It is a characterization that has been applied across the board in the mainline, now oldline, Protestant churches. In an effort to get a handle on this faith and ethos, I described it to myself as "civic faith." Civic faith holds both the greatest strengths and greatest weaknesses of the mainline churches.

For civic faith, the mission of the church is to ameliorate the human suffering of the city and to be the moral conscience of the community. The church, in this understanding, is a center of civic life, one that provides an avenue by which the most fortunate and powerful can be of help to the less fortunate and least powerful. Such a church seeks to embody and carry religious meaning for the civil society. The church, in this perspective, is part of the larger reality of Christendom, American style, which rests on the assumption that ours is in some sense a "Christian" society and nation. It was for such a church and such a faith that my own growing up in the Congregational Church and my educational background had prepared me. There are real virtues in "civic faith," including the emphasis on service, the concern for the life of the broader community, and the attempt to relate Christian faith to the life of the society. But increasingly the world for which this was an appropriate model no longer exists.

In the late twentieth century we live in a remarkably pluralistic society with a host of religious options and worldviews. Christianity has been disestablished and exists in a society that is somewhere between indifferent and hostile to it. It has become both presumptuous and impossible to think of oneself as *the* conscience of the community or as *the* carrier and embodiment of religious meaning for civil society. Today we may be a voice at the table, but we are no longer the host. Still less is it our table.

For downtown churches, the old "firsts" of every mainline denomination, there are additional changes and challenges. The economic and political elites began moving out of the city centers in the 1960s, and many have also moved away from the churches. It is no longer incumbent upon members of the social elite to be church members. Meanwhile, the social policies of recent decades have resulted in a concentration in the cities of the least fortunate — the chronically mentally ill, people with AIDS, the homeless poor. They are for urban congregations no longer "out there." The least fortunate are today themselves members, fellow travelers or frequent claimants on the resources of urban churches. In addition, the community beyond the church's doors is a much more heterogeneous one — ethnically, religiously, and in life-styles — than that envisioned by civic faith.

But the more serious challenge now faced by congregations and clergy is that they are often not well prepared or equipped to respond to what *does* bring people to a church in the last decades of the twentieth century. The people I see seeking a church today remain interested in helping others, but they are also spread thin and exhausted by the demands of work and family. What brings them to church are their own religious questions, their spiritual longings, their search for meaning and for God. Often they are unchurched or little churched and are eager for study and deepened understanding. Often the catalyst for their coming is a crisis — divorce, substance abuse, the loss of a job, a death or suicide in the family, an experience of depression. Often when such people come to a mainline congregation they are met with a litany of the world's needs or problems and the expectation that they will shoulder them. But as one woman said to me recently, "I give all week in my work and in my family. On Sunday I need to receive something. I don't need, at least every week, to be reminded of my responsibilities. I do need every week to be reminded of God's grace and presence."

This is a different world from the world of civic faith. In that world we tended to assume not only that ours was a Christian society but that most everyone was a Christian and understood what that meant. But this tended to be a "lowest common denominator" understanding: "Christians are nice people who help others." Being a Christian meant being a caring person, a good citizen, and one who was on the side of decency and social betterment. But in a religiously pluralistic world such definitions are too thin, too superficial, and too moralistic. In many congregations people began to ask, "How do we differ from any other civic-minded group?"

17

In many historic civic faith congregations, the best expressions of that ethos, with its strong impulse toward service and concern for the whole society, had given way by the 1970s and 1980s to a "gone to seed" variety of civic faith. The "gone to seed" variety was characterized by the sacrifice of most all historic norms and legitimate sources of authority — especially Scripture and tradition — to the authority of individual experience and personal preference. Increasingly it seemed that the task of the ordained was to adjust the gospel, Scripture, and tradition to people and their perceived needs, rather than assisting people in the process of being transformed in the light of the gospel. Social and political positions and actions of the churches were increasingly underfunded as theological roots and connection were lost or neglected. The peculiar language of the church was often sacrificed in attempts to speak the language of the culture. Frequently there was a sense of embarrassment when people spoke openly of God or Jesus. A "don't ask, don't tell" policy came to prevail in matters of personal faith.

When the consultant said, "You have a Christian in the pulpit. A lot of people are troubled by that," I suspect it reflected a growing dissonance between my post-liberal convictions and the more relativistic expressions of civic faith. I had come to believe that the Christian faith has an actual content. I had come to believe that a central task of the church and of the pastors and teachers of the faith was to form and sustain people as Christians. I had come to see worship as the beating heart of the church's life and the Scriptures as essential to the formation and inspiration of a people.

It is not easy to say exactly when or how this had begun to change for me, to say when or how I became restless with civic faith and concerned that it seemed thin, inadequate to the task, and ill-suited to new realities. In many ways that process began long before I entered seminary in the early 1970s or was ordained in the latter part of that decade. It had something to do with the string of national traumas and tragedies that took place in the 1960s and 1970s, when I was a teenager and young adult — the assassinations of the Kennedys and King, the horrors of Vietnam, the tragi-comedy of Watergate. At the very least, these events showed the inadequacy of liberal progressivism and its claim that the world was getting better and better. All of these traumas resulted in a vastly diminished trust in institutions and authority in any form. They drove truck-sized holes through the sacred canopy in which mainline churches, public schools, scouts, and service clubs were the key strands in a unified web of meaning, order, and purpose. As these traumas gave way in the 1970s to a widening drug culture, a catapulting divorce rate, and hyper-inflation, I came to believe that the challenge many people faced was not — as the liberal consensus held — to be free of tradition and authority, which were always construed as oppressive. Rather, it seemed that many sought something solid to stand on in the midst of modernity's constantly shifting sands. In the face of betrayal by presidents, parents, and institutions, some rejected all authority and tradition. Others sought new and more reliable sources of authority and direction.

In the fall of 1973 I entered Union Theological Seminary in New York. I found that seminary life in the seventies was geared more than anything else to equipping future clergy to be agents of change. The image of the church imparted to us then was that of a great sleeping giant. Our job as clergy was to give the sleeping giant a swift kick and motivate it to make America a better place by dealing with racism, sexism, capitalism, and militarism. Initially this excited me. But before long it began to seem thin, presumptuous, and moralistic in its own way. More than that, it seemed out of touch with the reality of people's lives and the church.

The churches I was coming to know — inner-city congregations in New York City and rural congregations in upstate New York — were anything but sleeping giants. As my friend Will Willimon puts it, "Here were people holding on by their fingernails, barely able to survive. And their survival needs were not merely financial. They were theological. We didn't know why we were there. We wondered how being in the church was different from being in any other merely helpful human organization." Seminary education in the seventies seemed predicated on the idea that rousing the great, complacent sleeping church was the name of the game. But the reality beyond seminary was a church and culture in crisis, desperate for meaning, with increasingly few clues about what to tell the kids, and reeling from shattered trust.

I began to develop answers concerning how the church was different and to find resources for a deepened faith in the Scriptures. My post-liberal turning has had much to do with the Scriptures. In the civic faith world in which I grew up, the Bible and its stories seemed mainly to be treated as texts of moral examples. The Scriptures were often used as ornamental attachments to already arrived at conclusions and convictions. Preaching was often the reminder of what all right-thinking citizens already knew. And amid all this the impression was unmistakably conveyed that the Bible was an incoherent relic, one that we had outgrown but kept around because we weren't quite sure what else to do with it.

When I actually ventured into the world of the Bible I found it surprisingly different. How anyone could reduce this to moralistic tales was beyond me! As often as not, God seemed to prefer working with sinners rather than saints. And in the Bible most people turned out to be both — sinners and saints — with the worst sinners being the ones who were convinced they were the saints. I discovered that while the Bible is a diverse and messy book, it has an overall wholeness and coherence, almost all of which points to a God who is intent on messing up our settled worlds and opinions and calling us into relationship with mystery. Most of all, I found that the Bible's texts and stories were not about to lie there inert and passive, awaiting our interpretation. They were alive and eager to have their say, if we could but muster the courage to listen. In my earliest preaching ventures I used the biblical text as, at best, a resource. But dissatisfied with that, I quickly changed and came to see the biblical text as source more than resource. I stopped asking anxiously, "What am I going to say?" and started asking, "What is the text trying to say to us, and to do with us?"

A further step in my post-liberal turning came when, as a seminary student, I accepted a position as a student assistant at a small, African-American congregation. Here I encountered people who spoke freely and without embarrassment about their faith. "These people talk about Jesus and they seem to mean it!" I reported with astonishment to my wife. I found this both compelling and alarming. I began to see how important the language and stories of faith were in forming and sustaining an identity strong enough to resist the corrosion of a prevailing cynicism and of the omnipresent market.

It was also in this congregation that I discovered the power of worship and experienced worship as the time and place in which one was met by the living God. Here the words of the Westminster Catechism about the chief end of man ("to glorify God and enjoy God forever") began to make sense. Worship was enjoyable. I began to long for it. But this was odd. My civic faith background, as well as my seminary classes, rested on the assumption that all the really important stuff happened beyond the church's walls, that what really counted was getting out in the world and in the streets. I began to suspect that we were getting out in the world, but without much notion of what to say or do as Christians when we get there, and not much strength or staying power to do it with. In this congregation I began to understand the link between worship and mission. I found worship to be an experience of both delight and danger. You would be met there each Sunday by the Risen One, and there was no telling what might happen.

After graduating from Union in 1977 I returned to the Northwest and began serving my first congregation, a smaller church in the foothills of the Cascades in western Washington State. It was in these years that I first became aware of the designation "mainline." But there was irony in this. For I also realized that if "mainline" meant roughly the center of the theological spectrum and in some way representative of the religious ethos of the society, we "mainliners" were not it. In the small towns and suburbs of Seattle the Assembly of God was probably closest to the mainline. But it was confusing. Our church sat proudly on main street, all dressed up for a part that we were no longer asked to play.

There I began to form another conviction that has also shaped me as a minister. I noticed that members of the congregation who shared a civic faith perspective had not much interest in Christian formation or in the teaching ministry of the church. We seemed to believe that everyone already knew what being a Christian meant.

We operated on the unspoken assumption that one could be a Christian without training. Our approach to new members seemed to be, "We just need to get these people on a committee, involved in some project, and they'll be fine."

With some exceptions, our model was that education was for children, while worship was for adults. This paradigm had come to prevail in many of the mainline churches. Later, in somewhat more sophisticated congregations where civic faith had gone to seed, a teaching ministry was problematic in a different way. The self and one's own experience were sovereign. Truth was to be found by turning within, not by becoming part of a community or being formed in and by a tradition. I began, however, to form and act on the conviction that recovery of the teaching ministry was crucial and that being a minister today meant being a teacher of the faith.

And something new was stirring. Some people, often younger people in their twenties and thirties, seemed to be yearning for faith formation and for ministers who were teachers of the faith. This was something that the burgeoning new conservative churches were only too happy to provide. Para-church Bible studies, meditation centers, and prayer groups were springing up everywhere — everywhere, it seemed, but in the mainline churches. We were busy with civic and community projects. But it began to seem true to me then, and continues to seem true, that mainline congregations were expecting people to bear faith's fruits while giving too little attention to faith's roots.

In the early 1980s I accepted a call to a multiracial congregation in Honolulu located near the campus of the university. I had gone to that congregation with the hope and expectation of rebuilding a church that at one time had numbered over seven hundred but had now, after a series of difficulties, sunk below two hundred members. And a fair number of the remaining two hundred were not on very good terms with one another! Added to this was the challenge posed by two dozen homeless persons who had taken up residence on the church's grounds. Over time I discovered that these were not the free-spirited sixties types that many imagined them to be. They were persons experiencing mental illness, substance abuse, or both.

Neither the congregation nor I was adequately prepared for such a consuming challenge. My inherited theology, with its heavy emphasis on shouldering the problems of the world and fixing them, met its match here. A cloud settled over my life that brought with it difficult learning and a further push beyond my received liberalism and civic faith.

A year into that pastorate I suffered a serious depression that lasted two years. At first I didn't have any idea why I felt so overwhelmed and debilitated. I couldn't imagine what was going on. Understanding, treatment, and learning came slowly, but they came. Part of the learning called for a different and deeper kind of faith, one that put less responsibility on me, and one that taught me of God's grace, and learning to trust the Spirit's leading. I came to see that I, like many churches shaped by civic faith, had turned a religion of grace into a religion of good works and achievement. We preached grace, but it was hard to receive it ourselves. In crucial ways this loss of a religion of grace, and its replacement with a religion of good works and activism, was destroying the mainline churches, even as it had contributed to my own terrifying experience of depression.

There were days, weeks, and even months when God seemed utterly absent, but there were regenerative forces at work. Something new was coming slowly to birth. I found my way, in those years, to a retreat center run by a couple of elderly Maryknoll sisters. They taught me how to pray the Scriptures, how to make a retreat, and how to receive spiritual direction. Stubbornly I disregarded the offhand advice of a psychiatrist to change professions. I came to learn the truth of St. Paul's words, "My power is made perfect in weakness" and "My grace is sufficient for thee."

I not only began to forge a new and more fully lived theology; I began to understand better the dynamics of a great shift going on in the role and place of the mainline churches. At that point I happened to read John Gardner's study *On Leadership*. The founder of Common Cause, Gardner described institutions in denial: "Motivation tends to run down, values decay. The problems of today go unsolved while people mumble the slogans of yesterday. Group loyalties block self-examination. One sees organizations whose structures and processes were designed to solve problems that no longer exist. If regenerative forces are not at work the end is predictable."

This seemed to me an apt description of the plight of the mainline churches in the 1980s. Denial was deep at all levels of the church. Slowly I came to realize that this was a large, complex problem, one that I would probably spend the rest of my ministry somehow addressing. But I had also come through my own struggle with depression to recognize that regenerative forces are at work, sometimes because of us, sometimes in spite of us. I came increasingly to see that one way to face the demons within the churches I knew and loved was to face them within myself. I also began to sense that one of the best ways to bring about change is to go ahead and act on your best hunches, intuitions, and convictions, to live into the new reality that is breaking into the midst of the old, and not wait for permission or consensus to emerge.

How then do I find myself going about ministry today? What constitutes a post-liberal agenda? What of the civic faith inheritance do I continue to value? What emphases do I now have in ministry that I would never have imagined when I walked out of Union Seminary and was ordained twenty-one years ago?

I would never have imagined that I would be thinking about, and trying to find ways to talk about, conversion. But I am. So much of mainline Protestantism has been focused on accommodation, on adjusting the faith to us, to so-called modern sensibilities, and to the world's version of reality. But we have given too much away. And in the process we have made the faith and the church awfully boring.

So I find myself returning to biblical language that has to do with change, with turning, with new life and new beginnings — "repentance," "new hearts and new minds," "dying and rising in Christ," "being born anew." I am not much interested in fundamentalist versions of conversion, which seem to me too privatistic, too scripted, and too inclined to present Christian commitment as the end of suffering or problems, when it may be the beginning of them. But more and more I believe that new hearts and new minds are the level to be working at, and this is the level at which many in our congregations long to be addressed. They are waiting, I believe, for their ministers to say, "People, something is at stake here, something that makes all the difference in the world."

A congregation's worship is crucial. Too much worship in mainline churches today is just trivial. It proceeds as if "it's just us folks here," and too often that's exactly what it is. There is a diminished sense of God's presence, of worship as risky engagement with a peculiar God. Too often we clergy seem to construe our role as that of protecting our congregations from this God, from God's holiness and grace.

I continue to find value in educational programs focused on social and political issues, but I try to push us to reflect on such concerns as Christians, drawing on Scripture and tradition to do so. While I am mostly a lectionary preacher, I do continue to address issues of social justice and community concern, but I try to speak as a Christian and as a teacher of the faith. I try to avoid the predictabilities of liberal or conservative agendas.

No longer, however, do I see the teaching ministry of the church as primarily in the business of providing information, a few interesting ideas you might want to think about. The teaching ministry is in the business of conversion, in the process of formation. Too often adult education in the church has been all electives, all side dishes. Today I am eager to focus on the main course, the core curriculum of church life and study aimed at helping people to become Christian and at sustaining the church as a peculiar people.

The civic faith agenda of service remains important, but it needs an overhaul. Too often the community service and social action agendas of the church have degenerated into do-gooderism. Service and advocacy ministries today need to be faith-based. Cut off from faith's roots and the ability to articulate why, as Christians, we are doing what we do, we won't do much. For all the talk in most mainline denominations about "peace and justice," I am not sure that much is really going on. I want more public witness, not less, but I want to see it as the practice of discipleship and as part of the whole of worship, teaching, Christian community, service, and witness.

I never expected to be in love with the Bible, but I am.

I never imagined I would be encouraging people to reclaim spiritual practices like Sabbath keeping, but I am.

I never expected to be talking with people who say something like, "I want to have a spiritual life. How do I begin?" But I find myself having just that conversation more and more often.

I am learning that when people in my congregation say something like, "I have trouble with Easter," I don't need to try to fix it for them by explaining it (and often explaining it away). More and more I say, "Gee, that's great. Easter is tough. It's troubling, all right. It may require change. New hearts, new minds. But don't worry, with God all things are possible."

With God all things *are* possible, even the birth of a new church out of the death of the old.

Up from Liberalism

WILLIAM H. WILLIMON

I suppose it seems strange for someone like me — a white, Southern male — to speak of my life as a process of growing out of liberalism. My formative years were in the segregationist, American South. In those years, as the civil rights movement was just taking form, and our world was getting ready to be rocked, we were told that "liberal" referred to someone from the North who wanted to force us into a new world through legislation. Liberals wanted us to change, and why change when one is reasonably satisfied with the world?

Only later did I awaken to realize that we are *all* liberals. That is, we have been trained to believe that we are the center of the world, a world where all significant insights and information are self-derived — in short, a world where there is no God who speaks other than ourselves.

Look at the way I have begun this essay. There is that little but revealing word, "I." Liberalism assumed that the world is something I construct, through my choices. In the liberal world, for the first time in history, humanity was promised that we would not be forced to live out some story imposed upon us from the outside by the church, or by our parents, or by our village. Now, as Stanley Hauerwas notes, we can choose our stories. I can live out any story that I choose. In fact, for the first time in human history, the very essence of humanity comes to be defined in terms of choices. The fullest human being is the one who lives life by the maximum use

27

of choice. To live the free, undetermined life is the goal of liberalism.

Yet, as Hauerwas notes, we are coming to admit that *this is also a story that I did not choose.*

The idea of some free, autonomous, undetermined individual is a fiction. As the great theologian Bob Dylan has said, "everybody serves somebody." Each of us is busy living out lives that are socially derived, a gift from a past, a product of a culture we did not choose, including liberalism. Liberalism claimed to create people who were autonomous individuals, free to choose and to fashion their own undetermined lives. And yet liberalism failed to see that this also is a story, a story at least as old as Descartes and Locke, a story imposed upon us by the culture into which we were born. The question is not, as liberalism thought, how can I live a life free of external determination? The question is, which brand of external determination will rule my life?

This is the culture to which the North American church chose to adapt. This is the culture into which I was inculturated. It came to me first in the form of American Christian pietism. Religion was a personal affair. It really didn't have anything to do with "politics." Christianity was some sort of purely personal transaction between me and Jesus.

When I got to college, I thought that I was in rebellion against this point of view. I learned that most of the important things that needed doing in our world were political, power issues, matters of agitation for enlightened legislation. I learned that there was a disjunction between the faith as Jesus proclaimed it and our pietistic individualism.

I was excited by the notion of Christianity as a means of rebellion against tradition and conviction, since I was, at nineteen, in a rebellious mood myself. I was later to discover that my very rebellion against tradition and convention was a way of demonstrating how utterly conventional I was. It is no rebellion against North American culture to believe such articles of faith as "history doesn't matter," or "we are the first generation to have lived on the face of the earth, therefore we must make up the rules as we go." This is standard stuff of the conventional liberal point of view.

In seminary, in my better moments, some good teachers gave me an appreciation for the subversiveness of the tradition, the way that the Christian tradition has of unmasking our ideologies and giving us visions we would not have had if we had been left to our own devices. I also began to learn what happens to a church that bought into the essentially liberal mind-set. For one, liberalism had a way of going limp. It failed to muster the necessary energy for sustained, significant social change. Once the first goals of the civil rights movement were achieved and the fight became more complex, the issues more stable, many of those who were earlier so strongly committed lost interest. People got off the bus on the way to protest and into their hot tub with Chablis. Individualism is a hard habit to break.

Growing up in the South, one thing you get to experience first-hand is sin. All Southerners, at least those born before 1960, believe in original sin. The everyday experience of life in a segregated society, in which a vast social evil was not only tolerated but also defended, gives one a great appreciation for sin. Daily you see otherwise good people do some dreadful things and call it right.

Liberal Protestantism tended to have an inadequate appreciation of our sin. Sin was too often attributed to a lack of information or a failure of communication. As a white Southerner, I knew better. The wrong that needs making right was more serious than the need for better social legislation or a more enlightened set of attitudes. What's wrong with us is deep, impervious to rational modification. Something more radical is needed if there is to be true change. It distressed me that artists, gifted novelists like Flannery O'Connor or Margaret Atwood, were more honest in their assessment of the human situation than my own church. No wonder our much-praised attempts at liberal social activism went limp. Our situation in our sin was considerably more serious than we had been led to believe in countless sermons on the essential goodness of people and the possible perfectibility of humanity.

A church that cuts itself off from its tradition is a church that has severed itself from the very sources whereby it might be renewed. Most of the sermons I heard in the sixties, and many of those I began to preach, took a superior, arrogant attitude toward the tradition of the church. A biblical text was taken and then mildly ridiculed, set aside, and some other more contemporary or acceptable solution to our problems was offered in the sermon. We lurched from one trendy social issue to the next. We subtly laid aside the notion of the church as the gathering of those who were trying to follow Jesus and presented the church as a gathering of like-minded people who are seeking to live vaguely better lives, who are committed to certain amorphous values like "justice," or "affirmation," or whatever else the culture happened to be infatuated with at that moment.

Furthermore, I came to see that many of the notions of church in which I had been imbued in the sixties were imperialistic and anachronistic. My image of the church was that instilled in me by the two-thousand-member church I grew up in during the 1950s — a stable, secure-looking fortress that was designed to look more like a bank than a House of God, appearing eternal, fixed, socially and culturally significant, the kind of building God would build if God had the money. If this church had a problem, it was that it was a great sleeping giant. My task as a new preacher was to kick this vast sleeping giant in the seat of the pants, to get the church motivated to make America a better place in which to live.

And yet, when I encountered my first churches in rural Georgia and South Carolina, they were anything but sleeping giants. Here were people holding on by their fingernails, barely able to survive. And their survival needs were not merely financial but also theological. We didn't know why we were there. We wondered how being in the church was different from being in any other merely helpful human organization. Many other human organizations care. So the church said something like, "But we care even more." There were other organizations that wanted to make our communities better places in which to live. So the church said, "But our care is motivated by *spiritual* reasons." All of this wore rather thin as we moved into the "me-ism" of the eighties.

As a young pastor I quickly learned that, though I had modeled my ministry on the notion of the minister as the agent of change, I was not offering my people resources that were adequate for them to change. I was acting as if the problem were lack of information or the need for more sincere motivation. The problem was deeper. The challenge was to find some way of being in the world that enabled us to be new people. I was trying to *improve* the world, rather than radically to *change* it.

Furthermore, as a pastor I became impressed, in my day-to-day pastoral work, with the depth of the level of my people's need. Their need was not for some mere modest modification of behavior; rather, it was for some way of putting their little lives in some larger, transcendent perspective. They needed not more rules, not more moralistic urging to do better. They needed God. They didn't need a world improved; they needed a new world. They didn't need more improvement; they needed salvation. Conversion. Detoxification. Liberalism wasn't wrong in seeking change; it wanted too little change. Something more was needed.

Sensing the limits of liberalism, I was helped by the thought of people like Will Campbell, Stanley Hauerwas, Clarence Jordan, Jacques Ellul, Richard Neuhaus, and William Stringfellow.

In my day-to-day pastoral work, I came to see that Flannery O'Connor was right. We are in a serious situation. Our problems are deep. If it is up to us to save ourselves, then we are utterly doomed. If there is not some gracious God who is able to reach in and save us, then we are without hope. Something was needed from outside our closed little liberal world.

Such were the first steps on my ascent out of liberalism.

That great fortress-like First National Bank of God church where I had grown up as a child was now on the ropes. In the space of about two decades, that once seemingly secure Protestant Christian hegemony over American life was ending. In my adult lifetime, mainline Protestantism had been disenfranchised, our liberal way of describing the world discredited, our cultural significance lost. The mainline had become sidelined.

Now, one biblical metaphor spoke to me more than any other — *exile*. Yes, that was us. What we once called home was no longer there. Now, pushed to the periphery of a culture of consumerism and violence, the mainline church seemed rather pitiful still making its periodic pronouncements to Congress, still acting as if it enjoyed a monopoly in American religious life, still adapting itself to a world it thought it controlled. The laity knew better, even if we clergy clung to the notion that the church was still the sleeping giant.

New thinking was required, some bold way of making sense of loss and disestablishment while at the same time daring to dream of a new world where God is. In exile Israel had dared to name its national disaster as a time of judgment on its past infidelity and as a time of promise for a new God-given future.

Might this be a similar time for my church?

Scripture: Our Home in Exile

At a committee meeting in the congregation one of us serves, the members were reflecting on the changes that have taken place in the worship of that congregation in recent years. "It just feels very different," someone commented. A number of others around the circle nodded. Someone else added, "But if you were to ask me for specifics, it would be hard for me to come up with any." A third person chimed in: "I know one specific difference. Now we read the Bible *every* Sunday." Before the pastor had time to express surprise at that comment, the first person who had spoken said, "Now, Harriet, you know that we have always read the Bible every Sunday. But now it is just so noticeable. The Bible seems to be *everywhere* these days."

Variations on this conversation have taken place in our congregations of late. The Bible does seem to play a different role in our worship and in the life of our congregations than it did a generation ago. The reading of Scripture has always been an integral part of Christian worship, but today the sermon, often based on the lectionary texts of the day, is not as likely to wander out of earshot of the biblical text, and scriptural imagery tends to ripple through the liturgies. Bible study groups of various kinds are also sprouting up, not just in the sleepy corners of a congregation's programmatic life, but closer to the center.

This development should not be surprising at a time when it is becoming increasingly evident that our culture is not even vestigially

Christian. Old Testament scholar Walter Brueggemann has observed that it was during times of exile that Israel became a textual community. Living as strangers in a strange land, Israel's very identity as a people was threatened, so they read and listened to stories to remind them of who they were and where their true home was. The novelist Flannery O'Connor made a similar point when she observed that the richest traditions of Southern storytelling began to flourish only after the Civil War. When a community of people is no longer in charge, when the more corporeal sources of identity are vanishing, the community turns to its texts and stories as wellsprings of life. Surely this is part of what we are observing in our churches today. It is now becoming clearer that the scriptural story is our home in exile. That is why the Bible seems to be "everywhere" in our churches these days. Now that the world no longer provides such an accommodating home for the scriptural community, Scripture has become our home.

It can seem especially odd that pastors in the Reformed tradition should have to "rediscover" the centrality of Scripture. After all, that is in large part what the Reformation was all about. The Reformers concluded that the Catholic Church of the time had vested tradition, particularly as it was represented by the office of the Pope, with exclusive authority. They challenged the authority of tradition by invoking the authority of Scripture. The Reformers' battle cry was "sola scriptura." They affirmed that it was through "Scripture alone" that we could come to know God.

Within the liberal church of the first half of this century, such debates came to seem almost quaint because neither tradition nor Scripture was thought to hold much authority. Instead, the focus of liberalism had turned to the insights and experiences of the individual. Naturally, this had particular appeal for modern Americans because we take ourselves more seriously than anything else.

Occasionally this assumption of the authority of the self becomes startlingly clear, such as during a discussion of the death penalty in a congregation one of us served, in which someone said, "I don't know what the Bible says, but let me tell you what *I* think . . ."

In many ways we still nurture our young people in this faith in the self, the preeminent value of our individual insights and experiences. In that same congregation the climax of Confirmation Sunday has been the moment when the young people who are about to be confirmed read their individual statements of faith. In those statements the confirmands share with the congregation what they believe (and do not believe) about God, Jesus, and the Holy Spirit. Typically, some statements are somewhat stumbling attempts to capture these enduring mysteries, while others are remarkably articulate; some express a budding faith, while others could only be called statements of doubt. The congregation responds to each with the lavish appreciation and praise of a parent who has just been presented with a child's first drawing.

One year, when the statements were particularly eloquent and most seemed to bear a startling resemblance to the God who is worshiped in that place each Sunday, a member of the congregation said, without irony, "After listening to those beautiful statements, God must be feeling especially good today" — as if the God who hung the stars in the heavens and set the earth in its orbit had spent a sleepless Saturday night anxiously awaiting the verdict that would be rendered by a group of fourteen-year-olds the next morning!

Gratefully, there are signs that our liberal infatuation with ourselves — our own insights and our own experiences — is beginning to lose its grip on us. Many, including the three of us, have become increasingly tired of our own insights and yearn for something more. It is now clear to us that our own understandings that arise out of our own experiences are not enough to sustain us. They are little more than a cup of bouillon, not substantial enough to nourish us for the long haul. We respond to Goethe's observation that those who do not draw on three thousand years are living hand-to-mouth. And so we turn to Scripture for insights that are beyond anything we might come up with ourselves, for a word that does not come from our own experience but instead reshapes our experience.

Nevertheless, when there is talk in liberal circles about the authority of Scripture, people get nervous. Liberals often begin discussions about Scripture and its authority by making sure that they distinguish themselves from fundamentalists. (Indeed, it is telling that our forebears were most concerned with being labeled a heretic, while many today most fear being mistaken for a fundamentalist.) Today there seems to be an almost frantic search for a way to read Scripture without lapsing into fundamentalism.

One such attempt is the renewed interest in recent historical-critical studies of the Bible. We have noticed, however, the irony that historical-critical studies of the Bible, often seen as an antidote to the dreaded fundamentalism, actually have much in common with fundamentalism. For both, the authority of Scripture derives from how the words got onto the page. Fundamentalists claim that the words of Scripture are authoritative because they come directly from God and therefore are to be read literally. Those who put great stock in the historical-critical method of study, such as the members of the "Jesus Seminar," use a more selective literalism — they vest with authority those words that scholars deem historically accurate.

For us, however, Scripture derives its authority not only from how the words got *on* the page, but also from how the words get *off* the page. That is, we believe that the best way to test the validity of the sayings of Jesus found in the Bible is to try to live by them! The greatest test of Scripture is the ways in which it has the power to shape faithful lives. This understanding was captured in the remarks of a student, an African-American man, in a seminary course one of us taught. The man said, "The one who made Jesus real for me was my grandma. She did that in a way that all of this scholarship cannot do. She just told the stories and lived the faith. Sometimes scholarship helps me better understand this Jesus my grandma introduced me to. When it doesn't, it fails the 'grandma test.'"

There is a distinction, after all, between news and Good News. One is reported in the magazines (perhaps even scholarly journals), and the other is proclaimed in lives like Grandma's. If we had to choose between the two, we would go with Grandma every time.

It is not that questions about the historical accuracy of what is recorded in the Bible are uninteresting but that often they are little more than interesting distractions. We remember hearing about a gathering at Yale Divinity School in which scholars were engaged in a discussion of the historical basis of the story of Jesus feeding the five thousand. They took up every scholarly tool — redaction criti-

36

cism, form criticism, historical criticism — and fashioned them as weapons to be used in the long and vigorous debate. When they had exhausted the debate they turned to theologian Paul Holmer, who had remained silent through it all, so that he could weigh in on the question. He said, "Well, while you were talking, I was just thinking that if Jesus could feed all of those people, maybe he could feed me."

We try to imagine what William Shakespeare would make of a scholarly debate about which play was written first, Richard III or Hamlet. After listening to scholars debate the question at length, we can imagine the Bard saying with exasperation, "Don't you get it? It's a play. Just do it!" So too, we imagine what Jesus would make of the seemingly endless debates about the historical accuracy of his words. "It's a movement, people! Join it!"

Recently Martin's congregation was host to a pastor from the Pentecostal Church of Chile. The Pentecostal Church has a partnership relationship with the Massachusetts Conference of the United Church of Christ. Pastor Oscar Aguayo came for a year as a missionary to the fallow mission field of Massachusetts. In the course of the year the congregation learned much from him about the demands of this faith we share. Pastor Aguayo's church survived the persecution of the murderous Pinochet regime. As a pastor he works daily with parishioners who struggle to have enough food to eat. He organizes the people in his neighborhood so that they can obtain fresh water and learn the basics of personal hygiene to stem the spread of contagious disease.

During the last month of Pastor Aguayo's stay, Martin's congregation hosted a conference on "What the Holy Spirit Is Saying to the Mainline Church." Attending the conference were representatives of mainline churches and others from Pentecostal churches in Boston and Chile. At one point, Harvard professor Harvey Cox, criticizing the work of the Jesus Seminar, said, "Can we finally admit that the historical-critical method and our preoccupation with the historical Jesus have taken us as far as they can?" To which Pastor Aguayo replied, "That would be a good thing. Then perhaps we would be able to preoccupy ourselves with the presence of Christ today."

It is telling, we think, that the kind of historical-critical study of

Scripture that is promoted by the Jesus Seminar just would not play in the barrios of Chile. In such a setting, all of this preoccupation with historical-critical studies of Scripture, all of this supposedly high-minded speculation about the historical Jesus, seems glaringly beside the point, like another Northern Hemisphere luxury and indulgence. For Oscar Aguayo, Scripture is a living story that is being acted out in the life of his congregation. It is interpreted through faithful lives. When Scripture is read in that context Oscar Aguayo sees a different Jesus — demanding, powerful, uncompromising, alive and at work among his people. Much of modern biblical scholarship not only fails the Grandma test; it fails the Oscar Aguayo test as well.

Paying attention to how words get off the page means, in part, recognizing that the Holy Spirit has a continuing role in how Scripture takes life. It is read in community, the community we call church, because that is the Spirit's primary residence. It is read, not in isolation, but in conjunction with the saints of the church, who provide our best insight into how that word can take shape in our own lives.

One result of the almost exclusive focus on how the words of Scripture got on the page is that it ignores the ways in which Scripture has been read across history. There is a tendency, in both fundamentalism and modern liberal scholarship, to read Scripture in historical isolation. Such readings evidence concern only about the scriptural accounts and us, as if nothing of interest or value has happened in the intervening years. G. K. Chesterton called tradition "the democracy of the ages." By paying attention to the ways in which Scripture has been interpreted and lived out in other times we draw on more than our own limited insights and widen the conversation to include the Christian church throughout history. We need not be limited by the insights of the current century, because we read this story in conjunction with others who have been part of the ongoing community of faith over the centuries.

Of course, this is not a popular notion among those who cling to the liberal beliefs in progress and individualism. One member of the Jesus Seminar likes to say, "Who came up with the biblical canon, anyway? It was just a bunch of bishops. There was not a scholar among them!" What is revealed in such a comment is the tendency of modern scholarship to read Scripture in isolation from any ongoing community of faith. That is why we believe it is important to affirm again that the Bible is the church's book. It was intended to be read, and lived out, in the community of disciples called the church. We think it is important to take into account not only the ways in which Scripture is read by individual Western scholars in the late twentieth century but also the ways it has been read across time and setting by faithful people who have endeavored to live by the scriptural word in community.

At stake in the way we approach Scripture is the question of whether anything outside of ourselves will be given authority over the self. To be sure, even Scripture can be enlisted in the service of individualism when it is read in isolation and retrofitted to comport with contemporary sensibilities. Indeed, the authority of the individual in our time is so largely unquestioned that it is assumed to be simply the way things are, which may be the worst kind of tyranny of all. But when Scripture is read as a whole within a community of faith that attempts to live by it, it has the power to free us from the tyranny of the self. That is why Scripture is playing a different role in the life of our congregations these days. It is our home in exile within a land where the individual reigns.

Before William Muehl came to preach at the first church Martin served he asked if the pastors of the church followed the lectionary in their preaching. At the time, Martin was a recent graduate of Yale Divinity School, where Muehl taught preaching for four decades, so his question prompted no small amount of dread. Martin assumed that Muehl, a good Episcopalian, would fear for Martin's homiletical soul when Martin had to tell him that the custom of that congregation was to let the preacher choose the text of the day. When Martin told him this, however, Muehl replied, "Good, now I can preach on something I really believe."

At the time, Martin was relieved to hear his professor's response. He also believed that a text of his own choosing would give rise to a sermon of more vitality and conviction. Martin figured that if he were particularly engaged by a text, then it would be easier for the congregation to be engaged by it. If the text were one to which the preacher's heart responded, "Amen," then the preacher would have a better chance of crafting a sermon to which the people would respond, "Amen."

Now all three of us use the lectionary as the basis for our preaching. We have come to see in Muehl's comment the most compelling reason for using the lectionary. After all, the sermon is not primarily a chance for the preacher to expound what he or she believes. Rather, the sermon is an opportunity for the preacher to give expression to what the gospel proclaims.

The lectionary helps both congregation and preacher understand that what the preacher says in worship is not what he or she chooses to say, but what the preacher has been told to say. All of us — preacher and congregation — stand under the authority of Scripture. The sermon is not a time for the preacher to say those things that he or she thinks we need to hear; it is a chance for us all to consider what God thinks we need to hear through the words of Scripture.

When Tony was a student at Union Theological Seminary he served a little Scotch-Irish Presbyterian congregation in upstate New York comprised mostly of dairy farmers. "I'm a bright young guy," he thought. "These people will be interested in what I have to say." But somehow they weren't all that impressed with a twenty-five-year-old from Union Seminary in New York City. They'd seen his type before. They said, "Here, preach on this," and handed him the Scripture lessons for the coming Sunday.

At first, Tony was offended: "You don't want to know what I have to say?" They patiently explained, "No, not really. What we want to know is, is there a word from the Lord? You see, life is tough here. Our neighbors and friends are losing their farms. Inflation is killing us. There's no work here for our young. They have to leave. No, we don't expect to learn all that much from a privileged twenty-five-year-old. But you go over there and sit and listen to the Scriptures for us. Listen and see if there is a word from the Lord."

Tony was tempted to respond, "A word from the Lord? Are you crazy? What is this?"

"This," the members of his new congregation might have answered, "is church. This is what church is, people created by the Word, people sustained by the Word, people who wait for a word from God. We're not all that interested in you and what you have to say. Our need is too deep for that. We need God."

We owe much to our experiences in those congregations that ushered us into a strange, new world, into a peculiar people who seemed to take God more seriously than they took themselves.

Recently Will was reminded of how strikingly countercultural such an approach to Scripture can be when he met with a group of students at Duke Chapel. He invited them to ask questions about why the congregation at Duke Chapel does what it does in worship on Sunday morning. To warm them up he asked, "Which act of Sunday worship do you find the most strange?"

One student answered immediately, "It's when, just after we all get there, there is that big parade . . ."

"You mean the procession?" Will asked.

"Yeah, the procession, and at the end of the choir, just before the clergy march in, somebody always brings in that great, big book."

"The Bible?" Will asked.

"Yeah, the Bible. And she always puts it up there and opens it, then looks at the preacher as if to say, 'There. Work from that.'"

At first Will wondered why that particular aspect of worship struck the student as "weird." Then he realized that her observation was perceptive, indeed. After all, nothing like that is happening elsewhere on campus. That hundreds of late-twentieth-century people should gather to hear from an ancient, disordered book from another time and culture and approach such a book as if it had authority over our lives *is* weird. Subversive, even.

Most modern Americans would prefer to take their religion a la carte, to choose what is pleasing and conforms to our view of life and leave the rest. Using the lectionary is a powerful way of saying that this is not an option. To be sure, there are other ways to recognize the authority of Scripture without using the lectionary. But when the preacher chooses texts on which to preach, the focus ends up being on the one doing the choosing. So we have found that the lectionary is a powerful way to emphasize week after week that the message we bring in the sermon is not of our own choosing, that the focus of our preaching is not on us or our own insights, but on the story that has been entrusted to us to share.

Walter Brueggemann has said that the preacher who chooses his or her text often will set up a situation in which the text and the preacher are allied against the congregation. The preacher says, in effect, "This is what the Scriptures and I think you need to hear today." But when the preacher is "forced" to preach on a particular text, the preacher and congregation sometimes can be allied against the text. The preacher did not choose a text and then lay it before the congregation. Rather, a text has been given to both preacher and congregation. They approach it together.

Both preacher and congregation may have difficulty accepting or living under the word that has been given to us. There are some truthful messages to which we are not yet prepared to respond, "Amen." As one person prayed after hearing a particularly troublesome passage read in worship, "Lord, we have heard your word this day . . . and we don't like it!" If the Scripture for the day presents a real challenge to our thinking or our way of life, there are times when the preacher will want to join in such a prayer. But we did not choose this word. If we believe that Scripture is in some way God's word to us, we have no choice but to grapple with it in all of its grace and all of its challenge.

Before we began using the lectionary we would write our sermons only after a careful exegesis of the text. But the preacher who approaches sermon preparation in this way begins with the assumption that he or she already knows something about what the text means and its relevance to the gathered congregation. That is, after all, why one would choose it. The lectionary, however, often presents the preacher with passages whose meaning and relevance are not immediately clear. This means that the preacher usually has to spend more time with a text before knowing what to say about it. She or he can expect to pace around more and chew off the ends of more pencils. This is simply the price one pays for approaching a text with fewer narrowing assumptions. The resulting sermon, however, often benefits from the excitement of fresh discovery, a process in which the preacher then invites the congregation to share when the sermon is preached.

One reason we use the lectionary is that we have learned to trust Scripture, when read as a whole, to form a faithful people. In response to the question, "Is the Bible true?" we would point out that the Hebrew word that is translated as "truth" implies a rich array of related meanings, such as "trustworthiness," "steadfastness," and "faithfulness." We approach the scriptural story as true in that it can be trusted to reveal God to us and to equip us to serve God in the world. Indeed, we have come to conclude that learning to trust the scriptural story in this way is more important than our conclusions about the historical accuracy of individual passages. If we allow ourselves to immerse ourselves in the biblical world — learn its language and let ourselves be shaped by the sweep of the story — our understandings, and indeed our very lives, will be richer than if we simply choose texts that appeal to us or prove our points.

William Placher describes well what it means to enter the biblical world:

> The Bible lays out a richly diverse vision of the world, from beginning to end, and says, in effect, "This isn't some imaginary world, like Tolkien's Middle Earth. This is the real world, the only one there is. So, if you buy into this basic picture of things, then anything real has to fit somewhere into this framework. Your life and the events around you thus will make sense only as they have their place within this grand story." ("Is the Bible True?" *The Christian Century*, October 11, 1995, pp. 924-28)

Obviously, for anything like this to happen we must immerse ourselves in this story and the world it creates. In short, we have to entrust ourselves to this story.

But why should we put our trust in the scriptural story in particular? When we enter what Karl Barth called "the strange new world of the Bible," we discover an alternative world that, over time, we can recognize as more real than the reality that is fashioned out of our own insights and perceptions. When we read Scripture, not simply as a book to be studied, but as a living story in which we are invited to take our part, it keeps making sense out of our lives. When we allow ourselves to be formed by this story, we find that it answers questions that we would not have thought to ask and in ways that we could not have imagined. When we ask of Scripture not only "What does it mean?" but also "What are we to do?", it keeps piecing our fragmented lives together in rich and surprising ways. When we approach the scriptural story as the ongoing story of the community of faith, we can not only recognize the ways in which it can fashion a new world but also experience the ways in which it can re-create us.

Discerning readers of the Bible can expect to encounter some passages that do not fit within their understanding of the world and others that simply seem unbelievable. We all have files in our minds labeled "Accepted" and "Rejected," and faithful readers of Scripture may be no exception. But those who entrust themselves to the scriptural story also have an active file labeled "Awaiting Further Light." Such a file will include many items that we would be inclined to put in the "Rejected" file were it not for the voices of historic Christian witnesses who have commended them to us. So we listen carefully when they seem to say to us, "Don't be so quick to reject this. You may not fully accept this now, but please trust us enough to put it somewhere where you will be sure to consider it again. In the meantime, why not try trusting this word enough to live by it?"

Those who actively use the file labeled "Awaiting Further Light" exhibit humility before the testimony of the community of faith. This does not mean that we must pretend to believe things we do not believe. But it does mean that, at certain points, we take the Bible more seriously than we take ourselves. It means freely recognizing, along with Shakespeare, that "There are more things in heaven and earth . . . than are dreamt of in your philosophy." It means that we dare trust the scriptural story more than our own limited perceptions. It means that we recognize that the question of what we can believe is not nearly so important as the question of whom we will trust.

Preaching and Speech:
Words Make Worlds

Because we are all three preachers, we are in the business of words. We have given our lives to the proclamation of the gospel, the nurture of the church's language, and the use of and care for words.

Church involves lots of talking. This is not only because we human beings are incurably linguistic creatures but also because, according to Scripture, the primary way the God of Israel and of the church has attempted to relate to the world is through speech. Our story begins in Genesis with God speaking: "Let there be light." And there was light. At the speech of God, chaos is pushed back, darkness becomes light, and world is born.

Israel is born through the word. On a starlit night, Yahweh pointed old Abraham and Sarah toward the stars and promised them that a great people would proceed from them, even though they were "as good as dead" (Heb. 11:12). Through the promise of God a people is created, a family is formed.

So, at the beginning of the story of Jesus, when John the baptizer preaches and his words are mocked by the religious establishment of the day, John tells them, "God is able to raise up children from the stones in this river if God needs to" (see Matt. 3:9). God has formed a people out of nothing, on the basis of God's word, and God can do so again.

The church is that amazing gathering of people congregated on the basis of nothing more than words.

George Lindbeck, Yale theologian, has noted how the church defeated the greatest empire the world had ever known without firing a shot, without lifting a sword. Rome was defeated, in the space of just over three hundred years, on the basis of nothing but a rather disordered conglomeration of writings called Scripture. The church was that countercultural phenomenon which gathered people out of the empire on the basis of the word. Rome knew no means of community other than family name, gender, social class, or military might. The church showed that it was possible to form a people on the basis of the word. Words.

When we began our ministry, we thought we knew what it meant to bring the gospel to speech. Basically, Christian proclamation involved evoking certain religious experiences within people, reminding people of what their best natures already knew.

This approach certainly characterized most of the preaching we heard during our formative years. The preacher begins with some aspect of the human condition — say, that we feel empty and are searching for something, or we want to make a difference in the world and don't know where to begin, or we all suffer from a lack of self-esteem. Then, moving from this contemporary assessment of the human condition, the preacher rummages about in the riches of Scripture or church tradition and applies some Christian truth to our contemporary situation.

When such sermons worked, they were wonderful. They demonstrated that the gospel was relevant, which liberalism thought to be the great test of the gospel. All truth is tested by its ability to help people in their present circumstances without any real critique of their assessment of their present circumstances. Our best liberal sermons surprised people by demonstrating that the Christian tradition, though very old and locally limited, still had something to say to our contemporary concerns. The role of the preacher was to be the skillful explicator of the contemporary human situation, the astute applicator of the faith of the church to our contemporary concerns, the one who spoke to people's needs. At their worst, however, our liberal sermons merely mirrored what was already being said by a variety of social, political, or psychological commentators who had the advantage of being able to comment on the "modern human condition" without all that superfluous God language.

Early in our ministry, we came to question some of the assumptions upon which this view of preaching was based. We learned through our experience in the congregation that words had a more complex function than we first imagined.

A book that influenced all of us early in our ministries was Fred Craddock's book on preaching, *As One Without Authority*. Craddock told us preachers what we should have known already. In contemporary North America, the old sources of authority have eroded. No longer can someone stand up in a contemporary pulpit and say, "The Bible says that . . ." and have it be the end of the discussion. If a preacher says that, the congregation replies with statements like, "The Bible is an ancient, pre-modern book. What does it have to do with us?"

It seemed that the contemporary preacher could not appeal to the authority of Scripture, church, tradition, or ministerial might. In today's world there is only one sovereign authority — me, mine, and myself — the trinity of philosophical liberalism. (Liberalism has always been ruthless in its rejection of any claims of authority or truth other than its own.)

Therefore, we were told, the preacher must preach inductively rather than deductively. The preacher must begin with human experience, with our common, everyday experiences of God's grace and judgment, and work from there. The preacher artfully evokes our experiences and then moves to show people that the gospel really is about those experiences.

As we have said, this was the preaching upon which we had long been nurtured in the mainline, liberal church, so Craddock's words struck a chord with us. Long ago Harry Emerson Fosdick, the father of American mainline preaching, told us that people do not come to church on Sunday morning to inquire, Whatever happened to the Jebusites? They come for help with their everyday problems and concerns. So, start there and move back toward the gospel.

Craddock continued this line of thought in his subsequent book, *Overhearing the Gospel*. There, Craddock told us preachers that one of our major problems in preaching is that people have "overheard" the gospel. They have heard so many stories on the parable of the prodigal son that, when a preacher stands up to preach on it, the congregation groans, saying, "Here we go again." Therefore, the preacher's challenge is not to provide them new information, because they have already heard the information again and again. Rather, the preacher's challenge is to speak the gospel in a new, engaging, and invigorating manner so that people are enticed to make a familiar journey again in a fresh, contemporary way.

These two books were immensely influential partly because they confirmed a number of presuppositions of the liberal church: Each of us, by being fortunate enough to be born in North America, already knows the basics of the Christian faith. North America is at least a vestigially "Christian" country, where people get the gospel as if by osmosis. People already come with all the attributes they need to hear the gospel and to enact it. The preacher's task is simply to evoke, to enliven what people already know. The only source of authority is the sovereign individual. That individual must be appealed to, indirectly to be sure, based upon that individual's experience. Issues related to human fallibility and self-deceit are moot because we are basically educated, sensitive, and caring people who have overcome what we used to speak of as "sin." The gospel is basically a set of ideas and experiences that relates to the general human condition, as we define that condition, and is therefore universally available to all. That is, the gospel is a common human experience that is waiting to be artfully evoked by the sermon.

Interestingly, it did not occur to us to ask ourselves, "Where did we get the notion of 'common human experience'?" We failed to see how much theory, how many presuppositions we brought to our experiences. We assumed that the gospel merely wanted to speak to our needs, as we modern people define need, when the gospel may actually want to rearrange our needs, may have a countercultural notion of "need." Fosdick's preaching, and its heirs, assumed that we already had what we needed to define "the human condition," whereas we have come to see that we have no *Christian* idea of what the "human condition" is before we hear the gospel.

To be fair to Craddock, even though these themes struck a chord in us and our fellow preachers, he never again returned to these themes. Perhaps he, before we, discovered the limitation of construing the preaching task in this way.

George Lindbeck's deceptively small book *On the Nature of Doctrine* sent powerful tremors through our liberal playground. Lindbeck's lofty academic intent was to describe the way religion works in the life and thought of believers. In so doing he named our situation with disarming clarity.

Lindbeck said that, for most of his academic life, he conceived religion in the conventionally liberal way. Religion is a universally shared human experience. All people, in all cultures, tend to participate in an experience called "religion." Or, in the preferred parlance of today, all people express something called "spirituality."

Despite the universality of this experience, curiously, there is a myriad of different religions, diverse expressions of spirituality. Why is that? The liberal says that different religions are simply different human ways of expressing the universal human experience of God. Thus, the liberal may say something like, "I am a Jew, and you are a Buddhist, but, after all, we all believe fairly much the same thing. We are all headed in fairly much the same direction."

According to this view, a Hindu and a Christian differ principally in the way they express their faith. Down deep, once one peels away the different labels and the different terminology, the different inadequate modes of expression, both have basically the same experience. Religion is no more than our fumbling attempt to express the universal experience of God.

You have seen these books that purport to describe various "world religions" and that have lists under categories such as "Love in All Faiths," with a collection of statements about love in various religions. The implication is that all religions believe in love, even though they may talk about it in some different ways. Religions may naively presume that they are different, that they are obeying different gods, until the liberal academic interpreter explains to them how, essentially, they are all saying the same thing.

This is what Lindbeck called the "experiential/expressive" view of religion. According to this view, religion is a common human experience that different faiths express in different ways. The experiential expressivist, in confronting people of different faiths, longs to get beneath the labels, the rituals, and the terminology to that deeper, shared universal experience which each of these faiths is trying to express in its own limited ways. Thus, Norman Lear says that he conceives of religion as a great river into which flow different streams called Buddhism, Christianity, Hinduism, and so on. The individual streams contribute to that great river. The important thing is not the individual streams but the larger river.

One of the motivations for this way of thinking was to lessen the cognitive conflict between various religions. There is little need for conflict and misunderstanding between different faiths because, when you get down to it and peel away the peculiarities, all faiths are saying fairly much the same thing. So can't we all just get along?

This project has a long history in the development of liberalism as a philosophy. Exhausted by a couple of centuries of so-called "religious" wars and conflict in Europe after the Reformation, the Enlightenment sought some philosophical means of laying aside our various religious differences, which have led to so much conflict. Enlightenment thinkers claimed to have discovered certain "universal," common human values that everyone could affirm regardless of that person's background, religion, nationality, or neighborhood. The Enlightenment therefore uncovered values like "equality," "brotherhood," "love," etc. These values were alleged to be universal and noncontroversial. In the Declaration of Independence, drafted by that supremely Enlightenment American, Thomas Jefferson, Jefferson speaks of certain truths being "self-evident." Rational people who take the time to think these matters through will come to the common conclusion that there are "inalienable rights" which are universally valid.

Of course, one wants to say to Jefferson, if these truths were so self-evident, why did we fight a war over them? Why couldn't George III figure this out just by thinking about it?

We now know, here at the end of the twentieth century, that the modern, Enlightenment desire to find some non-conflicted, universally valid truths is an impossible hope. There is no non-conflicted knowledge. Nothing we affirm is neutral, non-conflicted, noncontroversial. Our differences are real and must be taken seriously. They cannot be obliterated by denying them or by claiming that our truth claims are "self-evident."

What liberalism hoped to do was, in effect, to say that the differences between religions do not matter, which was really another way of saying that religions do not matter. What matters is finding some neutral, universally affirmable, philosophical standpoint that everyone can affirm and that will make conflict impossible. Thus, liberalism urged us to embrace alleged universal values like "human rights," or "values," or "justice."

What liberalism did not admit was that it had not solved our differences, but suppressed them. Religious people were forced to lay aside the distinctiveness of their faith traditions to embrace liberalism. Liberalism had not provided us a neutral, merely procedural way to deal with our differences. Rather, it had told us to ignore our differences and to embrace a different "religion" called Liberalism. And, as Lindbeck indicates, there is a sense in which we are all liberals in this society.

This point of view is demonstrated by the person who calls a preacher up and invites the preacher to offer a "non-sectarian prayer" at the first city council meeting of the year. The expectation is that the preacher will come and talk about "God" or "love and justice" or some other noncontroversial, neutral category that will not cause trouble among people of different points of view. Part of the arrogance of liberalism is its failure to acknowledge that this also is a point of view! Why should this point of view be privileged over orthodox Christian faith or Orthodox Judaism?

Recently one of us was asked to give the baccalaureate address at his alma mater. If it were not so painful, it might be downright humorous to witness the lengths to which a liberal institution, such as a college, will go in the attempt to vest such a ceremony with meaning after it has been stripped of its religious meaning. The college felt that it had to write a rationale for baccalaureate, so they sent a statement to guide in the sermon preparation:

51

Although Dickinson College is a place which values individuality and diversity, it is also a community which celebrates a long and distinguished history of liberal arts education. The Baccalaureate service, as the opening ceremony of graduation, celebrates our participation as a community in pursuit of a Greater Good, as it has been variously explored throughout the liberal arts tradition. There are many ways of comprehending what a Greater Good might be. But our graduating seniors and their families have invested a great deal (of time and financial resources!) supporting Dickinson's involvement in that tradition, and a commemoration of that very diversity that sustains our community seems an important starting point for graduation.

This, of course, is the kind of platitudinous language that fills many graduation speeches. In such settings the speakers reach for something BIG to say; but since God has been officially banished from the proceedings, they say something trivial about a scaled down, trivialized kind of god (Greater Good!).

When the preacher received this statement, he called the dean of the college and said, "I'm sorry, but you must have the wrong guy. I don't know anything about the 'Greater Good.' What I can do is tell you something about my God. Are people in a college that celebrates 'individuality and diversity' willing to let me speak as a Christian? Next year I would encourage you to invite a Buddhist, but if you do, I hope you won't ask her to talk about the 'Greater Good.' If she talks about something she knows about — like, say, Buddhism — I might learn something!"

Of course, the reason that liberalism dominates and drives other voices out of the conversation is that liberalism is the air we breathe and the water we drink. One of us returned from a meeting with a renowned contemporary interpreter of the Christian faith, a member of the "Jesus Seminar," and told a colleague, "He is one of the nicest people in the world. Very open, irenic, and collegial in his conversation." Our colleague replied, "Of course he is. Liberals are always open, irenic, and affirming. Why shouldn't they be? They've won!"

When a liberal appears open, accepting, and affirming, the liberal is only acting out the truth that liberals are in charge. Liberalism is the dominant, domineering worldview in our society. It used to look like home to us, but now we view it as the host culture in which Christians and other people of faith are in exile. Again, we are using the term "liberal" not so much in the political sense of the dichotomy between "conservative" and "liberal," for we do not think those labels are worth much anymore anyway. Rather, we are using the term in the philosophical sense — in the sense of someone who believes that the individual is the sovereign unit of society, that there are certain universally experienced values inherent in all people everywhere, that there is no truth other than that truth which is self-derived, and that it is possible to find some neutral philosophical ground whereby all our conflicts between different points of view will be resolved.

Lindbeck's "experiential/expressive" preacher always begins with human experience, with some experience that is alleged to be part of the general human condition. The sermon begins by talking about depression (where did we get the word "depression"? Who uses that word? Who benefits from its use? What does the use of this description exclude? The "general human condition" is getting more and more difficult to find!) or by talking about our need to belong, or some other universally shared trait. Then the preacher goes to the Christian tradition and demonstrates how that tradition offers helpful resources for dealing with this common concern. A Christian is someone who has had an experience of God and has found the Christian faith a useful means of articulating that experience.

Lindbeck said that he had found that the experiential/expressive way of characterizing religion did not fairly or accurately describe the way it actually felt for people to be religious. You cannot erase the particularities and peculiarities of a religion and end up with that religion. Even the notion of "religion" is suspect; the notion of "spirituality" is even more so. Is it true that, if you really sit down and listen to a Buddhist, a Hindu, and a Muslim, you can come away convinced that those persons are basically having the same experience that you are having as a Christian? Once again, such a point of view is an arrogant refusal to recognize the real differences among people. It is the typical liberal means of refusing to take religion seriously as a valid way of construing the world.

We do not think that faithful Muslims or Buddhists are flattered by Christians who are quick to absorb their particular traditions into some larger whole. In fact, we are confident that devout people of other faiths would agree with us that this sounds more like religious imperialism in a friendly guise. Most often, when people say, "We are really saying the same thing," they really mean, "You must be saying what *I* am saying . . . just not as well."

Against this view, Lindbeck laid out an approach to religion that he called "cultural/linguistic." Being a religious person is somewhat analogous to learning a new language, says Lindbeck. To become a Christian is to enter a "culture," a complex system of rituals, words, signs, symbols, habits, and practices that make us who we are. Just as you cannot learn the French language by reading a French novel in an English translation, so you cannot get Christianity by having the Christian faith translated into some other philosophical framework like liberalism, or existentialism, or Marxism, or the language of self-esteem. Rather, to be a Christian is to be someone who has learned the language, someone for whom the "grammar" of the Christian faith has become part of your life.

The way in which you learn grammar is not by memorizing a book of grammatical rules. The way you learn to speak grammatically is to be immersed in a setting where words are used in a certain way. For instance, you come to know what "sin" means by hearing the word used in a variety of situations and contexts. There is no meaning of the word apart from the way it is properly used. To be sure, memorizing a grammar book takes less time and can be done in isolation. But to fully get the "grammar of faith" one must be a part of a community that speaks grammatically. It is a slow business, but there is no substitute.

Ultimately, of course, the church needs to be that kind of setting in which we can learn the "grammar of faith." Along these lines, one of us was touched by a conversation with a young person in his congregation. She said, "Of course, my whole life I have heard all the religious words in church. But this year I have begun to try them on for size. When before I would have used the word 'mystery,' now I try saying, 'the work of the Holy Spirit.' I have even begun to call certain evils 'sins'! I'm not sure I always get it right. I'm still trying these words on for size, but I think it's a start."

It takes time to be a Christian. It requires practice. You have to get the moves. You have to learn new words. If you receive the gospel translated into some other philosophical point of view, you have not received the gospel. You have not said "salvation" when you say "self-esteem." You have not said "God" when you say "ultimate reality" (Paul Tillich). To be in the church is to be in a culture, a counterculture. It is to learn a new language. It is to be in a new world.

Words make worlds. We can live only in a world that we can see, and we can see only a world that we can describe. As the poet Wallace Stephens observed, we live in our description of a place, not the place itself. Liberalism denied the disjuncture between the world of Christianity and the world of North American, capitalist, consumerist, violent culture. Through translation, it hoped to make the gospel more palatable to a late-twentieth-century culture. But this will not do. Christianity is more abrasive than that.

By the way, Christianity is not weird in that it requires conversion, or because it requires someone to take the time, the trouble, to submit to the words and the habits of the different culture. All "worlds" are like that. Even the world of baseball. *Especially* the world of baseball. Nobody on the face of the planet can go to a baseball game, uninformed, and expect to know what is going on. Baseball has its own vestments, rituals, rules, and language. If baseball is not "user friendly" and fully accessible and inclusive without training, how much more so must be the gospel of Jesus Christ!

In a recent discussion in a pastors' school, someone asked Will, "Do you really believe that Christians ought to try to go out and convert people?"

Will replied, "Absolutely! You are a member of the United Church of Canada, so there is a good chance that it won't work, but go ahead, show them your stuff, and let's see what happens!"

When this declaration was met with some resistance, Will replied, "If you don't want them converted to Christianity, what do you want them converted to?"

There is no "world" — self-evident, natural, normal — just sitting out there. Everybody lives somewhere. Everybody is standing somewhere. So in North America when you say, "I don't want to impose my point of view upon you, I don't want to convert you to Christianity," what you are really saying is, "I want to leave you alone so that capitalism, consumerism, materialism, and all the ideologies that control this culture can have their way with you. I am going to defer to those 'conversions' rather than attempt to convert you to Jesus." Why should we Christians do that?

We are learning that *it is all conversion*. What we first thought of as our humble, self-effacing attempt to articulate the gospel in a "responsible and contemporary way" was a simple demonstration that we had submitted to the powers-that-be. We had given up the battle too soon. In bending over backward to speak to the "modern world," we fell in. In our dialogue with contemporary culture, the traffic moved in one direction. It was always contemporary culture rummaging around in the gospel, telling the gospel what it could and could not believe. This is a project in which we have lost faith.

Words make worlds. As Walter Brueggemann has told us pastors, if we will not let the gospel use us to create a new world, then all we can do is service the old one. And that's no fun. All we can do is breathlessly run errands for the world, and in a consumerist, consumptive culture there are so many errands to be run. People become omnivorous pits of desire, grabbing and acquiring everything for fear they might miss acquiring the one thing that might give significance to their lives. Alas, we bring our children to church in the same way we take them to soccer practice. We think it will help them develop and that it will help them compete and mature in the world as it is. In such a culture, our strategy ought not to be to present the gospel as just another "something" to help give empty lives more meaning. Our strategy ought to be fundamentally to critique the very basis on which this world is constructed. That fundamental critique is called gospel.

For each of us this has meant an earnest attempt (experiential/

expressivism is such a hard habit to break!) to begin our preaching with the gospel rather than with our assessments of the "human condition." The gospel implies that we have no idea what the human condition is before we meet Jesus. In confrontation with Jesus, our notions about what human beings need are rearranged. Many of the things that we thought were our needs are revealed to be superfluous. Jesus does not always meet our needs. Rather, sometimes he gives us needs we never had before we met him. Jesus does not merely give significance to our lives; he utterly rearranges our lives. We come to Jesus, thinking that he is another means of helping us to feel better about ourselves, and he rearranges our whole notion of ourselves. Suddenly, our lives are not our own projects to do with as we please. We come to see our lives as commandeered, owned, claimed by God for God's purposes. We discover that we have a more interesting reason for living than ourselves.

In such moments we realize that the gospel is after bigger game than merely to "speak to the contemporary world," the project that liberalism assumed. The gospel doesn't want to speak to the modern world. It wants to *change* it. God's primary way of change is through words, by bringing a new world to speech. Thus, on Sunday morning, when the congregation gathers, we speak about things that the world tends to avoid. We talk funny. We use peculiar speech. Sunday morning becomes at times a conflicted, downright unpleasant place to be, because we are not merely renaming the human condition by the use of certain primitive, first-century expressions. Rather, we are busy moving people to a different world. We tell stories and lure people into a different citizenship. We reconfigure their notions of what is going on in the world. Thus, the people emerge from church, their eyes blinking in the sunlight. On Sundays when it's good, they emerge, not simply into the world at half past noon, but into a world where Jesus Christ is Lord, where the kingdom of God is beginning to take form, and where their lives are given significance as those who are ambassadors, emissaries, the first wave of God's promised kingdom.

Ritual and Sacrament:
Beyond Words

It was Ash Wednesday. When I [Tony] entered the sanctuary I noted a congregation, gathered that Wednesday evening, of about three hundred. This was considerably larger than the usual turnout for an Ash Wednesday service. The reason for this was no mystery. A concert of African-American spirituals was scheduled to follow the service itself. The artist, a member of the congregation's choir, had recently released a new CD of spirituals that had received an enthusiastic review only days before in one of the city's daily papers.

Looking out on the congregation, at least half of whom I had never laid eyes on before, I grew increasingly nervous. The publicity had been clear enough — an Ash Wednesday service would precede the concert. But what would this crowd make of an Ash Wednesday service, with its long confession of sin, Psalm 51, and mea culpas, and most of all the primitive ritual of smearing ashes on people's foreheads? Would they feel the church had played some kind of bait and switch game, trapping them with the bait of the concert? Members of the congregation's Music and Arts Committee were stationed at the doors of the sanctuary; after the service began they started to hold back those who came for the concert only.

I rose to lead the service thinking "My God" (yes, it was a prayer), "I had no idea there would be so many people here, so many people I have never seen before. Will they be put off by the service, even offended?" I decided a brief description of the service was in or-

der. I spoke of the origins of Ash Wednesday, the way it marks Lent's beginning, and the meaning of the ashes. Meanwhile, as the service proceeded, another three hundred people were crowding into the church lounge outside the sanctuary awaiting the concert. As they waited, conversations were struck up. One of our congregation's members at the door found himself speaking with several people who identified themselves as "Methodists."

"What's going on in there?" demanded the Methodists, pointing toward the sanctuary. "Ash Wednesday service," explained the congregation's man at the door. "Ashes on people's foreheads, beginning of Lent." "What kind of weird Congregational Church is this?" asked the Methodists. Proving a willing if unorthodox evangelist, our man at the door said cheerfully, "Our minister has introduced a lot of religious effects. Five years ago they would have lynched him, but now they love it."

His summary was blunt but accurate. What he dubbed "religious effects" we would call the rituals and sacraments of the church. But he was right about the congregation's likely response. Five years earlier the congregation would have had none of it; but these days people are finding new depth and meaning in ancient rituals and sacraments of the church.

That night, as people came forward to have the sign of the cross pressed on their foreheads in ashes and to hear the words spoken to them, "Turn away from your sins, and believe the good news of the gospel," it was astonishing that almost all of the three hundred did come forward. Even more, the pastors who anointed people with ashes couldn't help noticing tears in some eyes, a longing (for what? mystery? faith? forgiveness?) on many faces, and the unspoken meaning that each touch seemed to convey. It was a risky moment, and a powerful one.

Two nights later my wife and I were walking on a street in the center of one of the city's more avant-garde districts. The streets were crowded with hawkers and panhandlers, with twenty-somethings adorned with green or purple hair, and with people sporting a wide variety of pierced body parts. Suddenly, out of this crowd, a woman stood before me. "You're the minister at Plymouth." "Yes," I an-

swered cautiously, wondering what I was about to be hit up for. "I was at your church on Wednesday," blurted out the woman. "I want to come back. I'll see you Sunday." With that she disappeared into the crowd, the brief and unexpected encounter leaving me with a feeling of mystification like that sometimes caused by the rituals and sacraments. I was left, however, also with the sense that there is an Other at work in surprising and unexpected ways.

A quality common to rituals and sacraments is that they all provide the occasion, the language, and the gestures for people to encounter realities and truths that, left to ourselves, most of us would avoid. It is too scary. The truths are too deep, the language too powerful. The God who meets us is too surprising, too fearfully loving. But in providing the occasion, the language, and the gestures with which to approach this God, the rites and sacraments of the church are also a gift to us. They enable us to tell, to hear, and to act out the truth about ourselves and our world, and the truth about God, "whose ways are not our ways, whose thoughts are not our thoughts." They grant us a zone of safety for encountering truth, mystery, and the holy.

The choice before us today is not ritual or no ritual. Human beings will always have rituals of one form or another. But some rituals are better than others. The prophets of Israel, and Jesus as well, were critics of the rituals of their people. They pointed out that sometimes ritual served not to tell the truth, or to seek a deeper truth, but to obscure the truth about who we are and who God is. This is a persistent danger. Good ritual, like a good story, has elements of both safety and surprise. Good ritual both delights and disturbs. It comforts and it challenges.

By and large we have an idea of what to expect when we enter into the predictable pattern of a memorial service or a baptism or a celebration of Holy Communion. We may know the words and gestures well. There is comfort and security in that. Knowing this, we can let down our guard a bit; we can let go of some of our need to be in control. But in good ritual we are also surprised, disturbed, perhaps even confronted with truths we have not seen or felt before. As familiar as it all may be, we see something we have not seen before, hear something new. We see ourselves, others, our world, and God in a new way, and we are renewed in the process.

Rituals and sacrament seem increasingly important today. They have the power to sustain us in what we have come to see as a time of exile. As we ask ourselves why this is so, at least three themes emerge, three elements of the experience of rituals and sacraments that have been problematic for the liberal, civic faith world, but now seem important in a new time. One of these is that the rituals and sacraments of the faith tend to be particularizing. They separate those who participate from the culture as a whole. A second theme we note is that rituals and sacraments often put us in a vulnerable position. They remind us that we are receivers of grace, that God is God. Third, the rituals and sacraments of faith create spaces for our imaginations to roam and stretch, for the human spirit to rediscover the immense power that resides in symbol, image, and story which take us beyond the rational. They invite and permit a certain experience of "make-believe" that may be crucial for a people who would envision "a new heaven and a new earth." All seem important to us. All also seem problematic, even threatening, to the world of liberal and civic faith.

"This Is Different": Rituals and Sacraments Particularize

When one of us was a student at Union Theological Seminary in New York City, he registered for a class on "Worship." Early in the semester the professor, possibly in an effort to get to know his students, asked each of them to write down on a sheet of paper what were the "high, holy days" in their church tradition. At that time this student was largely unaware of seasons like Advent and Eastertide, or festivals like Pentecost, or rites like Ash Wednesday. Even Palm Sunday and Good Friday had not greatly impressed themselves upon him in his Congregational childhood and youth. What to put down on the blank sheet? Then suddenly he knew. The high, holy day of his Congregational tradition was Thanksgiving. Pilgrims, Puritans, parish hall suppers, pumpkin pies, and gratitude for being an American. When he dropped his slip of paper on the professor's desk, the professor, an African American whose own tradition was Pentecostal, looked it over and snorted, "Thanksgiving! You've got to be kidding!" But he wasn't. It was the great civic-religious holiday, with particular meaning to Congregationalists, but available to the whole culture. This national rite was *the* high, holy day, or so it seemed to him.

How did one of us travel from the civic holy day of Thanksgiving to the dark depths of Ash Wednesday? Though the impressions of youth may not have been wholly accurate, why did the civic holiday of Thanksgiving make such an impression, and why were other rituals and feasts held at a distance or completely unknown?

From a religious perspective Thanksgiving does have meaning, potentially quite profound meaning. For John Calvin gratitude or "thankfulness" was the origin point of ethics. Ethics, as Calvin understood them, were responsive in nature. They were a response to God's acts on our behalf and to God's goodness. For much of the Reformed tradition it is true, as someone aphoristically summed it up, that "salvation is all about grace, ethics all about gratitude." Yet, at the same time, Thanksgiving can be and often is celebrated with no particular religious element or perspective. Its significance may be limited to the patriotic, civic, or familial. It may even, in degenerate forms, become merely a celebration of affluence and consumption entirely adrift from larger moral meanings. But in all of these forms Thanksgiving remains a ritual that is widely available to the culture at large. It does not separate a person or family from the culture. Rather, the observance of Thanksgiving joins one to that dominant culture.

This is a clue to one reason for the minimizing of ritual and sacrament within the liberal and civic faith tradition. Ritual — from the Sabbath observance of Jews, to the Ramadan of Muslims, to the O Bon dances of Buddhists — tends to be particularizing. It separates one out from the secular, seemingly universal culture. It emphasizes difference. It requires that an explanation be passed, as at the Passover meal, from one generation to the next. To the outsider, ritual may appear "different," even "weird." Those who are anointed with ashes at a morning Ash Wednesday service run the risk of others thinking, or saying, "Excuse me, you seem to have something on your forehead," and finding themselves needing to explain their smudged face. Or when Communion is celebrated at a Christmas Eve service some will say they are "uncomfortable" on behalf of family or friends who "come for the music and feel excluded" by the sacrament. In a sense, they are right. The rituals and sacraments are strange. They tend to draw a line between believers and non-believers, insiders and outsiders. But they also reinforce the sense of identity of believers and offer to them depths and meanings not readily available in the host culture. Part of what it means to recognize that we live "in exile" is a willingness to demarcate, even separate, oneself from such a culture.

In this new era we can learn much from the Jews, who have long known the importance of ritual in maintaining their faith. One of us was reminded of this on one occasion when he and his family got a flat tire in the Bronx. He did not have a jack to change the tire and there was not a phone in sight. In that neighborhood tall apartment buildings loomed like fortresses.

Then a cab pulled over and let out a little lady who was stooped over as if she were carrying the burdens of New York. He approached her slowly, so as not to seem too threatening, and explained his family's situation. She invited him to use her phone.

When he entered her apartment he was introduced to two other stooped-over women. He called the towing service but found that the line was busy. He called every few minutes, and in between he had a chance to learn about the keepers of this oasis of human kindness.

He noticed a sign on the kitchen door saying that it was strictly kosher. He saw that the kitchen table was set with the Sabbath meal. One of the women kept saying, "I hope your call gets through before Shabbat (Sabbath)." Then it dawned on him: as traditional Jews, they will not use the phone after the sun goes down and the Sabbath begins.

Now the phone calls had a new urgency, but the sun was making steady progress and he was not. Finally he asked, "You will not use the phone once the Sabbath begins?" His three new friends

64

seemed to be startled by the question. One replied, "No, we will not make any calls and we won't answer the phone either." It was just that simple, and just as problematic for him, as that.

Then, perhaps sensing his reaction, she asked, "Are you a Jewish boy?" When he said that he was not a Jew but a Christian, all three women laughed and rushed to reassure him by saying over and over, "Oh, you can call. We can't, but you go ahead." They all laughed together. With that, the sun slowed down and the call finally got through.

As he left their apartment he felt grateful for these women, not only for the ways in which they had helped him, but also for the ways in which they faithfully maintained their religious rituals. Nothing in the modern world encourages them to do so, but their religious rituals and practices (another of which is hospitality to the stranger) make life in that hostile environment tolerable. Just as such observances have sustained Jews through exile and persecution, so now they sustain life and faith in urban America. There may have been a time when Christians in America did not need to tend to their own rituals so carefully. But that time has now passed. Thanksgiving is not enough.

There are many Christian rituals and liturgical practices that particularize: keeping Advent when the culture at large is doing its version of Christmas, keeping Sabbath in a world of relentless activity. One particularizing ritual of Christian worship that we have found significant is confession of sin. Calvin said, "Confession of sin begins with the house and people of God." In other words, there is evil in the world, but we are not equipped to battle it, or even face it, if we have not faced and done battle with the evil within ourselves and our own institutions. The confession of sin allows us to speak and tell such hard truths — truths about our broken lives and relationships, truths about our complicity with evil, about wrong done and right neglected. But confession does not end there. We are enabled to tell such truths, to abandon our self-justifications, because we have learned, as Christians, that we cannot justify ourselves, nor need we try to do so. We are justified by the grace of God, which is the context for confession of sin.

Nevertheless, in liberal and civic faith congregations we have served, confession has been a bone of contention. It draws a line in a world committed to self-esteem, to feeling good and being upbeat. To many people it seems "too negative," even unnecessary. It is something that will make the casual visitor uncomfortable (not to mention the regular member!). But Christians who share in this weekly ritual of confession and assurance may come to the understanding that we do not need relentlessly to accentuate the positive or cover over our own remorse and grief. As Harry Emerson Fosdick reminds us, "Mark this strange fact that the church is the only organization in the world that advertises itself as a company of sinners." We are freed to do that. We can face the negative, be truthful about our shortcomings, confess our sin. And only a person of faith can really do that and not despair, because we do not put our trust in ourselves, but in God. Confession of sin is odd in a society awash in blame, complaint, and self-justification. But this oddity may well be redemptive.

Surrendering Control, Being Receivers

Another reason for the minimization, even suppression, of ritual and sacrament in the liberal, civic faith tradition may be that ritual often puts us in a vulnerable position. As people file forward on Ash Wednesday they know they will be physically touched by another, that words — at once traditional and intimate — will be spoken to them. They know that in this moment they will be more receivers than givers. They will not be in control. This is an act of self-surrender to an Other, to a mystery that has touched and will touch us but that we cannot contain or control. This is difficult for people who are accustomed to being in control, who are used to being givers more than receivers, who prefer to think of themselves as self-made. Whether in baptism, in having your feet washed on Maundy Thursday, in the announcement of grace following confession of sin, or in the experience of being prayed for there is a yielding, a vulnerability that is unfamiliar and uncomfortable for many.

Yet, in another sense, such yielding, such receiving, such surrender of control may also be welcome. Many persons in congregations we have served give a lot, in a variety of ways, day in and day out. They care for others in their work and in their relationships. They are apt to accept high — sometimes unreasonable — levels of responsibility. They do not as often experience being cared for. Often they need help or permission to recognize the limits of their responsibility. Many serve and work in roles and positions that ask them to be in charge, in control, and to make frequent decisions. When such people are able to allow it, ceding power, even control, to God is a welcome act of faith and trust, an acknowledgment that we are finite beings. Perhaps above all, such experiences remind us that Christian faith is about grace. It is not first about our doing, but about God's doing. Before we are doers or actors, we are recipients. Salvation *is* all about grace; ethics *is* all about gratitude.

A sacrament of the church in which we are especially invited to surrender ourselves to God and God's grace and be receivers is baptism. One of us recalls an adult baptism where the candidate was a woman, a psychologist, who held a very responsible position in the community. She was in her mid-thirties, attractive, and took care with both make-up and clothing. The congregation had recently decided on using a greater amount of water in baptisms. As the prayer was offered, the water was lavishly poured out into the font. We were reminded that water is a powerful symbol of cleansing and refreshing. It is both life-giving and dangerous. It is playful and disarming. As he baptized the woman with a generous amount of water, he was horrified to notice her make-up running down her face, and her carefully done hair flattening out against her forehead. After the service, he apologized. She said, "No, don't apologize. It was really quite wonderful. Somehow I felt like a child again. Reborn." In that moment of being not in control, of receiving, she understood something powerful and central about baptism.

Several years ago the United Church of Christ joined other denominations engaged in liturgical renewal and revision by including services of healing in its new *Book of Worship.* Services and ministries of healing that had previously been suppressed or consigned to the margins in the Christian church are now reappearing. Such services and ministries may have been suppressed partly because of confusion about the biblical meaning of healing. (Often healing has been mistakenly equated with cure, when it can also encompass the restoration of personhood and place in community.) One important aspect of such services is the way they invite and permit people to say that everything is not all right with them, that they do need healing, that they do need grace, that they are not in control, even that they have failed. Such frank acknowledgments have not often been permitted in liberal, civic faith churches. There people have been encouraged to think of themselves as strong and gifted, ready and able to change the world (with a little help from God!). They are asked to be givers, not receivers. Not as often have they been invited to see themselves as persons in need of forgiveness, healing, or reconciliation — as receivers.

It is an act of courage for people to participate in a service of healing, to seek the laying on of hands, prayer for their needs or the needs of another close to them, or anointing with oil. The rituals of healing represent a powerful shift for the civic faith church. Such a church often speaks to what one might describe as our "noble self," our altruistic self. We are called to rise above our baser human instincts and to serve others. This is important. But at least sometimes our noble self is not our real self. It is a cleaned-up version that may have more in common with the self-righteous Pharisee in the New Testament than with those whose need led them to seek Jesus and find new life.

Every year one of us attends a gathering of about five hundred United Church of Christ pastors that is part convention, part continuing education, and part rest and relaxation. One year the theme of the gathering was "Ministry as Healing." The assembly heard sermons and lectures on the theme. The nuances of healing were debated. But then, after the sermon at the final worship service, the worshipers were invited to seek healing for themselves, healing of their own diseases of the body, of their brokenness of spirit, healing of memories or a relationship. After all, who knows, maybe, just maybe, there were one or two clergy who were themselves broken. Maybe, just maybe, there were some wounded healers in the gathering.

When invited to go to one of several stations set up around the ballroom-cum-worship center, stations at which requests for healing would be heard, foreheads would be anointed with oil, and a prayer for healing would be said, the room became so still you could hear the people around you breathing. For a long moment, no one moved. The worshipers had talked about healing all week, but this was something different. They were being called upon to seek healing through a specific ritual. But then one, and then another, person stood up. Soon long lines formed. Only a few remained in their seats.

That worship service lasted two and a half hours, although it was scheduled to last only half that long. Obviously there were wounds hidden beneath the suits and ties, the dresses and make-up, and behind the facile smiles. And that is reason for great hope. If the church has anything to offer the world, it is the chance to participate in and live out the death and resurrection of Jesus, to be healed in the broken places and claim a new life.

Beyond the Rational to Make-Believe

When one of us came to the congregation he currently serves, he was told by long-term members of the staff, "People at this church don't like Communion. Attendance drops by half on Communion Sundays." Communion was celebrated only four times a year, one of those being Maundy Thursday. Whether the claim that "people don't like Communion" was an accurate observation or a self-fulfilling prophecy is difficult to say. Reasons for such a situation and assessment may include some already suggested, but there is another factor at work. Sacraments and rituals are also acts of imagination that defy the Enlightenment and modern devotion to reason and to the rational. They invite, if not call for, a suspension of disbelief. They are not head first. They are often experiences of the heart, of the body, and of the senses. All of these are suspect in a world committed to the rational above all else. Experiences of the heart and imagination, body and senses, are something we both want and do not want simultaneously.

As children of the Enlightenment we have been schooled in reason, skepticism, and fact. If it can be measured, then it is real. We were not born yesterday. We are all from the "show me" state where what you see is what you get. If it seems too good to be true, it probably is. Surely these are useful lessons. But they are also cautious and reductionist ones. They discount or dismiss whatever cannot be explained. They are lessons that leave a certain emptiness and ache in the place where imagination is meant to reside.

Toward the end of John's Gospel Jesus says to Thomas, "Have you believed because you have seen me? Blessed are those who have not seen and yet have come to believe" (John 20:29). Jesus might have said, "Blessed are those who are able to make believe." For most of us "make-believe" is something children do and adults do not do, something like play. But make-believe, like play, is glimpsing and permitting a new creation. It helps us see more than the congregation eating the bread and drinking the cup. It allows us to see a new creation in which all find a place at the table, in which all are brothers and sisters. Imagination invites us to see in that meal more than how things "ought" to be. It also emboldens us to declare that what we see *is* how things really are. We are all connected in ways we seldom imagine. It is the imaginative act by which baptism is a torrent in which we are drowned and yet given new life as a gift. It is an act of imagination by which we are gathered with the faithful, alive and dead, on All Saints Day.

Not long after the fall of the Berlin Wall a thirteen-year-old girl, who had been forced into prostitution by her mother in the former East Berlin, found her way to a residential Christian community. She found shelter and a home there. She watched the community at worship. One day there was a baptism. The pastor spoke of being "born again." The words were, for this child, neither familiar nor formulaic. They were startlingly real and hopeful. Timidly, but with a faith that Jesus said is possessed by all who will enter the kingdom of God, she asked, "Can I be born again?" She was able to imagine a fresh beginning, a new life starting with baptism. In many ways, faith is an imagination that is free and alive — free to make believe and play, free to trust, free to believe.

Communion is a sacrament that, like all sacraments, moves beyond the rational. It invites us into another world. Perhaps one reason why some congregations experience a drastic drop in worship attendance on Sundays when the sacrament is celebrated is that our range of imagination has been too limited, too constricted. In some settings Communion is always thought of as a reenactment of the Last Supper, heavy with themes of betrayal, unworthiness, and sorrow. But not all celebrations of the Lord's Supper are celebrations of the Last Supper. That is to limit a sacrament of many meanings and tones to only one meaning and one tone. It is to constrict the congregational imagination.

To be sure, our celebrations of this sacrament are in part a solemn commemoration of Jesus' last supper. We take our place at the table of betrayal and death. But that is not the end of it — not by a long shot. There are times, at this table, when we close our eyes to picture again being in the dark, but the light is so bright that we can still see it. At such times it is as if God's imagination overtakes and infuses our own. We are invited to imagine that the story ends not with defeat but with triumph, not with Good Friday but with Easter. The meal itself is transposed from a minor key to a major key when it is celebrated with the risen Christ. Christians who gather around that table are invited to let their imaginations embrace the entire story. At such times, the sacrament becomes a resurrection meal.

This is a sacrament that invites our imaginations to flow in many different directions. At times we may be able to discern the Body of Christ in the congregation that gathers, in all its imperfection and beauty. Sometimes Communion is a foretaste of the kingdom itself, as was Jesus' feeding of the five thousand, where all ate and were filled. At other times we find ourselves eating with strangers and sinners, as Jesus did. We may be uncomfortable, but we may also find a gracious and surprising fellowship, one we may experience nowhere else. Not only do these different experiences of the sacrament, informed as they are by different parts of the gospel story, enrich and enlarge our experience of Communion, but they also spill

71

over into "ordinary" life. We celebrate a meal with friends and it somehow becomes more — a foretaste of the kingdom, a rich banquet of God. We eat with estranged family members and know something of Christ's power to heal as bread is broken and shared. We can come to see the world and ourselves differently because of this sacrament. Our imaginations are renewed and enlivened. The sacrament invites us into a new world that we can come to see is the real world, after all.

We all find our imaginations renewed, our minds and hearts stretched beyond the rational and reductionist, in other sacraments and rituals of the church. For us the Communion of Saints has become a source of great meaning, as the saints are remembered in the weekly liturgy of the church. All Saints Day has taken on new significance for some of us. In one of our congregations a "Book of Life" is made available six weeks before All Saints Day. The congregation is invited to enter the names of those who have died so that they might be remembered in the service. Four to five hundred names are entered, and each name is printed in the order of worship for the day. The names of all those who have died in the past twelve months are called out in prayer during the service, a service at which a jazz band offers music. It is a simple but powerful ritual. As the names are called out, as particular members of the congregation are summoned from the memories of the worshipers, it is as if the biblical "cloud of witnesses" gathers in the sanctuary with the congregation. A strange thing happens. The dead whom the congregation have come to honor and remember actually comfort and strengthen the congregation by their remembered stories and examples. Those who came to honor the dead are honored by them, and we come to understand the way the church transcends the ordinary bounds of time and space. Such is the element of surprise that awaits us in the rituals and sacraments of the church. As with most surprises, they can both startle and delight.

It seems important to say that for the most part we are not creating something new. We are working with what has been given to us. We are working with what we have inherited. We do not come to the rituals and sacraments of the church with suspicion as our dominant point of view. We are less in the business of creating something new than of discovering what has been overlooked or forgotten in one era of the church's life. New occasions do teach new duties, and moving beyond liberalism's civic faith may require that we remember what at times we have seemed happier to forget.

Christian Formation and the Teaching Ministry: Becoming Christian

At a recent biannual national meeting of the General Synod of the United Church of Christ, twenty-some resolutions came before the assembled delegates. The title of one was "Reclaiming the Role of Pastor as Teacher." In the committee that was deliberating on this resolution, one of us noted an interesting pattern. Most lay delegates seemed to support the resolution. "We need this," they said. Reservation and opposition came mostly from the clergy. They saw the resolution as one more expectation, one more thing to do, for their already overburdened lives and ministries.

At one point in the discussion a delegate rose to point out an apparently forgotten truth. "In this denomination the office of ordained minister is defined by the two words 'pastor' and 'teacher.' To be a minister in this church is to be a pastor *and* a teacher." The resolution was not calling the clergy to anything new, only to fulfilling their vows of ordination. Moreover, the wording of the resolution, "Reclaiming the Role of Pastor as Teacher," is revealing. Being a pastor — counselor, care-giver, crisis-manager, helper — was assumed and accepted as the central role of the ordained minister. Being a teacher of the faith was considered an option, an addition, something new.

"Pastor" and "teacher" define ordained ministry because they are complementary, parts of a whole. The teacher who is not a pastor, who does not know her people, their lives, their joys, and their sorrows, will be a teacher without the trust and relationships that make faithful teaching possible and fruitful. But the pastor who does not also teach, who does not bring the insights and resources of faith and tradition to bear in the face of human need, will be little more than another well-intentioned, helping professional. Such a pastor will be without the words that are life-giving and that are the difference between care and pastoral care.

The resolution, "Reclaiming the Role of Pastor as Teacher," and the discussion it provoked are symptomatic of the state of the church's teaching ministry in many mainline churches and denominations. When it comes to a viable teaching ministry and to the broader task of Christian formation there has been a failure of nerve on the part of the liberal and civic faith churches. To us it seems that a renewal of the church's teaching ministry, of the church as a learning community, and of the larger task of Christian formation is now essential.

At a congregation one of us serves, the only continuing adult education offering for decades was "The Forum." Each Sunday morning at 10:00 about two hundred people take their seats at the Forum to hear such speakers as university professors, newspaper editors, a former senator, the mayor, the superintendent of the school board, or another civic leader or expert. They speak on a social or political issue of the day. Often there are several-week series on a theme, such as education, homelessness, peace in the Middle East, or health care reform.

The Forum proceeds according to generally understood, but not stated, rules for civic discourse. Participants are to be polite, tolerant, and respectful of others' opinions. Both sides of a controversial issue are to be presented. Explicitly religious speakers and topics are kept to certain times of the year (Advent and Lent) and otherwise are frowned upon. Partly this is in keeping with the Forum's purpose — to address civic concerns and topics. But it also reflects a suspicion that the religiously committed may not be sufficiently open-minded for the Forum. The mission of the Forum is generally understood to be that of presenting information in order that "people can make up their own minds." Participants are implicitly promised, "You will not be told what to think or believe here."

In many ways the Forum is a great program. It connects an urban church to the city and its civic life. Knowledgeable people discuss issues and topics of genuine concern. The Forum is also a community service. And yet, the Forum audience has aged and declined. The Forum does best with the generation born before World War II. Somehow it appears not to be as successful in reaching the baby boomer generation, and it is even less successful with the baby busters (also known as Generation X), a segment of the congregation that otherwise has been growing. It was a great fit for the liberal, civic faith era, but it may not be a viable form for the church's primary adult education ministry in a new era.

In the era of the liberal, civic faith church it could be assumed that most everyone was, more or less, Christian. We lived in a seemingly Christian culture. Christian values and stories permeated our society. Most everyone, or so we thought, had the basics of Christian faith — the Scriptures, knowledge of worship, some practices of spiritual devotion, and Christian values. But, as we have said, we no longer live in that world and have not lived in it for some time. Today people do not have a grasp of the Christian basics simply by virtue of living in American society. Today there are many competing worldviews and stories about life's meaning and purpose. Today modernity and market forces ceaselessly erode tradition and the communities that are the carriers of tradition. Therefore, we believe that a primary task of the church's ministry today is to provide basic and accessible teaching of the Christian faith. In this new era congregations and clergy must think intentionally and clearly about how people become Christian.

Today that congregation still provides the Forum, but it has also added to its teaching ministry. It has come to think of itself as "a teaching church" and "a learning community." A core curriculum that runs in a two-year cycle offers basic faith education, including such classes as "Christianity 101," "Worship and the Sacraments," "Exploring the Christian Spiritual Life," "Prayer for Beginners," "Understanding the Bible," and "Christian Life and Practices." Other kinds of teaching and learning go on as well, and the congregation has come to think of worship as central in the work of Christian formation.

The Forum, as the sole adult education program, not only rested on the increasingly inaccurate assumption that people already have the basics; it also rested on another assumption characteristic of philosophical liberalism: the authority of the sovereign self. "We are not here to tell you what to think or believe" is a frequently invoked mantra in liberal circles. "We are here to help you make up your own minds, to choose your own values." It all sounds modest enough, but such rhetoric masks a great arrogance. "No wisdom or tradition or experience of the ages or of others can help you here. It's up to you — the individual — to decide what is true for you. It's up to you to choose your own values, create your own identity, choose your faith." The result is a world that is often — especially to young people — chaotic, arbitrary, and unreliable. It is a world where there is no truth, save the truth you choose for yourself. It is a world in which few if any relationships can be trusted, where there are no reliable authorities, where there is no wisdom worth passing on from generation to generation. Liberal and civic faith congregations often have adopted this set of assumptions. No wonder the church's teaching ministry has atrophied! No wonder clergy content themselves with being helping professionals! When the individual and his or her experience is sovereign, when there is no trusted tradition or valued authority or reliable wisdom, teaching and Christian formation become highly problematic.

In such an environment, governed as it is by assumptions that are so much a part of our culture that we seldom notice them, the church and the clergy have suffered a failure of nerve. Confirmation programs have been abandoned altogether in some congregations. In other churches, confirmation has been reduced to a time when young people make their decision for or against the faith. Rather than understanding confirmation as the word itself implies, as the marshaling of the congregation's resources to strengthen a young person for the perilous journey toward becoming an adult and a Christian, it has become a time when the congregation anxiously awaits confirmation by its youth. It is a sad irony that confirmation so often seems to be confused with graduation — and just when young people are at an age when they begin to be capable of assimilating Christian teaching!

In the area of adult Christian education, while there are signs of change, it has been true in many congregations that there has been no substantive teaching for adults at all. The prevailing paradigm has been that education (Sunday school) is for children and worship is for adults. This has been a disastrous split. As John Westerhoff has helpfully observed, it has meant that the church has educated children and nurtured adults, when we should be doing just the opposite. It has exiled children and youth from the worshiping community. It has meant that many adults cease their education in their faith at eighth grade or, often, much earlier. Why, even the Gentiles (the culture at large) understand the need for life-long learning! Only in the church have we imagined that biblical and theological understandings of a third grader would suffice for life.

One striking indication of the church's loss of nerve is that the church has failed to trust its own Scriptures, language, rituals, and the formative powers of the community of faith. One of us recalls the bewildered teaching team for the senior high class that came to him one fall. They explained that they had excitedly announced to the young people, "This fall we will be focusing on sexuality and self-esteem." The young people groaned. "Oh no, we get that in school. Please, no more self-esteem!"

"Do you think we could study the Bible?" asked the students. "This is the only place we have a chance to do that."

These young people had more hope for the church's ministry than their elders. They had eaten of the cultural pottage of "self-esteem" already. They wanted their inheritance — the Scriptures (which do, by the way, have quite a bit to say about sexuality and its distortions, about love and about respect of self and others).

The teaching team was bewildered not just because of this interest in the Bible, but because they were themselves ill-prepared to help a new generation understand and claim the Scriptures because they had never done so themselves. But, wonder of wonders, teachers and students learned together. Today it may well be that the part of the average congregation most in need of a substantive teaching ministry is not the children but the adults. As Clarence Jordan reminded us, you can't raise live chicks under dead hens!

We find that in this new world the assumptions of the liberal, civic faith era of the church no longer work. We have come to a new set of convictions that shape our practice of the teaching ministry.

First, we reject the idea that theology is an elite activity and an interest to be pursued only by experts, mainly in an academic setting. The natural habitat of theology is the church. Those who do theology are not only those who hold advanced degrees in that academic field, but all who are and seek to be Christian. Theology is not first of all an academic discipline. It is, as an older understanding of theology holds, wisdom proper to the life of the believer. It is a perspective, a lens, a way of seeing life that is shaped by the teachings, life, ministry, suffering, death, and resurrection of Jesus. It is a perspective formed by the stories of Scripture, an imagination furnished and fed by the liturgy and sacraments of the church. It is a way of seeing exercised by those who have learned the practices of Sabbath, hospitality, forgiveness, and discernment, to name a few of the Christian spiritual practices.

Second, we have come to believe that the teaching ministry of the church has less to do with information than with formation. As a society, we are big on information. We want to travel "the information highway." We understand that information is power. But some are beginning to suspect that information alone will not save us. In fact, it may kill us. We imagine that it will not be long before people are crying out, "Deliver us from all this information: from voice-mail, e-mail, bulk-mail, and call-waiting."

The church's ministry of teaching and learning is not primarily one of providing information *about* God or *about* Jesus or *about* Christianity or other religions. We are less interested in information than we are in formation. The church's specific task is to help people become religious or spiritual in the Christian way. We are in the business of people-making. We do not want only to teach and learn information, as if this were another interesting diversion or passing fancy. We want to form and sustain Christian persons and congregations as disciples, followers, of Jesus. We believe the church would do well to come clean, to drop the pretense of objectivity. We, too, are in the conversion business. If we do not make our best run at converting and forming our children, our neighbors, and ourselves, we can be sure that someone else will. They will become new-agers, or devotees of the sovereign self, or servants of material wealth or worldly success, or "survivors" who have no other ambition in life than trying to slip through. All such faiths, as well as others, are in the conversion business. The only thing that sets the church apart in this regard is that it has something better, truer, deeper to offer.

A third conviction we share is the notion that the primary teacher today is not the Sunday school teacher, the minister, or a parent. While all of these are important, the primary teacher, the primary agent of Christian formation (or malformation) is the congregation, the community of faith itself. Information may best be dispensed by an expert, but formation is best achieved in community. The whole church both learns and teaches. The church and everything it does (sometimes for worse as well as better) proclaims the meaning and practice of a way of life.

When we lived in a nominally Christian society and the church received tacit support from the culture (no shopping or soccer on Sundays, prayer and Christmas carols in the schools), the church was part of a society-wide pattern of teaching of religion and values. Today that's changed. The church of today is an outpost in a culture that is sometimes friendly, most often indifferent, and sometimes actively hostile to it. (One of us recalls the construction company that planned to erect a crane in the street outside the church, thus blocking access to the church, on an Easter Sunday not long ago. When it was pointed out that it was Easter, the New Jersey–based ownership acknowledged that they were unaware of that and, frankly, did not much care. They had a permit.) We do not long for a return to the era of American Christendom. We see our changed situation as one of exciting opportunity to be the church in new and more authentic ways.

The church is more an alternative than was true thirty or forty years ago. This means that how the church understands its life and relates to the world around it is a form of teaching. When we worship we are doing something different, something odd, for today atheism and passivity are the consensus options. Just to worship

81

faithfully is teaching an alternative. In such a culture, the presence of a worshiping community will require interpretation, to ourselves and to others, of what we are doing when we worship. This was not necessary when the church blended into the culture landscape more easily. Now, there are more people who will not assume that they already know what it means to worship, and specifically to worship the triune, Jesus-shaped, God. In a culture like ours, such an odd practice requires interpretation, teaching.

In our time the church has many such opportunities to teach through the peculiar ways it relates to the world. For instance, how does the church understand and treat strangers? Does the church see the stranger — as contemporary society does — as a threat, a danger, and a problem? Or does the church remember and embrace a specifically Christian and biblical understanding of strangers as guests who, at least potentially, bear gifts of their own that will be revealed and shared when hospitality is experienced?

We teach and learn in so many ways. As we sing the hymns of the church, we are also learning to pray. As we read Scripture on Sunday, the manner in which it is read and interpreted says volumes about what we mean by "Scripture" and how it functions in the life of the church. Our sacraments and our forms of service to our neighbors all teach. In this new world, in a world in which the church is a community of different stories, values, and vision, the congregation and its life are the primary teacher.

That said, it is also our conviction that ordained ministers must, once again, become teachers of the faith. Many models of ministry are available and observable today. Many clergy today are managers of the institution, keepers of its schedule and its resources. Success in this model is a busy church, a full calendar of activities, and a smoothly functioning organization. Another model of ministry is that of the helping professional, one who answers to any and all human needs. We are cheap therapists, amateur social workers, and all-around nice people. Success in this model is being needed. Of course, since human need is inexhaustible, success of this sort may kill you!

Another model of ministry, one we find both more appealing and more faithful, is more rabbinic in nature. Here the minister is a community-based teacher of the faith. She or he is steeped in the Scriptures, is able to speak and share the peculiar language of faith, and is able to help people envision and practice a way of life that is specifically Christian. One of us recalls meeting with the adult education board of his church as they planned offerings for the year ahead. They were preparing to send a survey to members to inquire what they wanted to learn about. When asked what he thought of the idea of a survey, he replied, "Well, I try to imagine a rabbi asking his congregation, 'What would you like to learn about this year?' That would not happen. Instead, the teaching of the rabbi is governed by the question, 'What do my people need to learn in order to become good Jews?'" The survey was scuttled.

Sometimes teaching will be formal and explicit — in sermons, classes, or writing. Often teaching will be more informal and implicit — in helping sort out a congregational conflict, in interpreting a personal tragedy, in framing a controversial issue in the community, in modeling certain practices and behaviors.

To be a teacher of the faith a person must be a lifelong learner as well. This, too, will mean formal study, through continuing education, reading, study, and mission-related travel. But it will also mean personal disciplines of study of the Scriptures, prayer, worship, and conversation about matters that matter.

Given these convictions, what are some of the strategies, the actual practices, by which we might reinvigorate a ministry of teaching and Christian formation? There are two broad categories of strategy we would offer: One has to do with a more formal and explicit teaching ministry. The second has to do with Christian formation and the way a congregation forms and sustains persons in the practice of Christian faith.

The Teaching Ministry of the Church

Over the years we have noted a pattern in the churches we have served. If a person becomes especially alive to the Christian faith, eager to learn and to grow, it seems almost inevitable that such a person will be urged to enroll at a seminary. "You really should go to seminary," members of the congregation and clergy will say. We are not so sure. We suspect that often people at this point are confusing conversion with call. They are confusing becoming Christian with a call to ordained ministry.

Besides that, we have been to seminary. We recognize all too well the truth of John Updike's veiled description of one prominent divinity school in his novel *Roger's Version*. In that novel the central character, a seminary faculty member, describes what happens in seminary: "We get students who are like cabbages — plump, moist, fragrant with the earthiness of an eager faith. By the time we are through with them they are like cole slaw — chopped, diced, sliced and dripping in a sweet and awful dressing."

We are not sure seminary is *that* bad, but neither are we entirely confident that it is the right place for every eager student of the faith. Moreover, we suspect that the frequent recourse to seminary on the part of those who are eager to learn more about the Christian faith masks a deficiency in the church, that there is often no ordered teaching ministry. There may be a scattered smorgasbord that reflects the particular preoccupations of the pastor, or the latest issue or author, but often there is little that is ordered, sequential, or intentional as the basis of Christian life and growth. To us adult education in many congregations appears all side dishes and no main course.

By "ordered learning" we mean to suggest that Christian faith does have an identifiable content and substance, that some themes and bodies of knowledge are foundational, and that some topics or subjects build on others. Most of all, we want to argue that congregations need to become communities of learning, providing opportunities for such ordered learning and expecting members of the congregation to utilize such offerings. In virtually every other field of interest today, adults expect to continue learning and sharpening their skills throughout their lives. People understand the idea that learning and study is sequential, that you do not begin with "Advanced Computer Programming" but with "Understanding Your Computer and Its Programs."

We would urge, in this new era, not only that congregations

embrace the concept of "ordered learning," but that congregations develop a "core curriculum." The key question in developing such a core curriculum is, "What kinds of knowledge and experience do people need in order to become faithful Christians?" Different congregations will have some variation in their answers and their curriculum. Earlier we shared the core curriculum at the church one of us serves. No core curriculum should be closed. Over time some things will be added and others dropped. But the point is that we can no longer assume that people get the basics of the faith by living in American society. We can no longer assume a knowledge of biblical stories, of the music of the church, of sacraments or worship, of Christian values or the long history of the church.

When a congregation takes seriously the ideas of ordered learning and a core curriculum, the question will arise, "Who is going to teach all these classes?" Our answer to this query is twofold. Although clergy may at first be reluctant, and not all have the gift of teaching, our experience suggests that, if clergy are given adequate preparation time, most will find teaching a particularly rewarding form of ministry. At the very least, we are confident that teaching is more what they thought ministry might be than many of the things to which most clergy give their time. But clergy cannot and should not attempt to do this alone. One of the tasks of the ordained is to help identify and equip laypersons who have the gift of teaching so that they might exercise their gift as teachers in service to the church. Both clergy and laity are called to be lifelong learners, and both are needed to carry out the teaching ministry as well.

Christian Formation

While ordered learning is critical for the church's life today, Christian formation also proceeds in other settings. In many ways, becoming Christian is less a formal and didactic experience and more an experience of relationships and community. What we have called "ordered learning" has an important place; but it is a part of Christian formation, not the whole of it. One way we have come to think about Christian formation more broadly is by looking at sports, crafts, and the arts. To practice any of these, there is some element of formal instruction and ordered learning, but there is much more to it than that. We think these practices provide crucial clues for Christian formation.

In becoming one who practices a sport, a craft, or an art, there are five identifiable, common elements. There is a set of skills, a language, a history or tradition, a master teacher or teachers, and a community of those committed to the practice.

In oil painting one must know how to hold the brush properly, and in baseball how to handle the bat correctly. In karate one must know how to stand or hold one's body so that the weight is centered. Each of these is a *skill* that must be learned. Through instruction and practice a certain level of proficiency is attained. We find that one place where one can acquire what might be called the skills of being a Christian is in worship. There we learn and weekly rehearse a set of skills or practices: hospitality, Sabbath, praise, confession, forgiveness, listening for God, offering, prayer, sacrament, blessing. Each of these skills is learned by doing and by observation. As we rehearse these skills weekly in worship, we prepare to practice them in our daily lives. They are a set of movements that together make up the dance of being a Christian.

Arts and sports involve not only particular skills but also a *language* specific to each. Different postures and movements in karate have different names. A baseball player must learn what is meant by "an inside-out swing" and "good arm extension." So, too, in the church we have a language to be learned. Some of our language is common in the world, but we have particular meanings in mind for words like "witness," "love," "forgiveness." Some of our language is uncommon and even threatening: "sin," "salvation," "grace." The first and natural habitat of such language is worship, the language of liturgy, Scripture, and prayer. By participating in worship we hear and may, in time, come to use the language in order to describe realities and experiences not available to us before.

Language is one element of a larger *history* or *tradition*. One learns about the origins and intentions of karate, about past masters of painting, or about the memorable games or players that define the sport of baseball. Many such activities have magazines and other publications whose primary function is to use the language and propagate the tradition. We sometimes speak of "passing on the tradition," as if it were a static thing. It is not. A tradition is a living thing. We find it useful to remember that the word in the Bible translated as "tradition" is a verb. It would be more apt to speak of "traditioning" a person. We see this going on as parents, teachers, and friends "tradition" another into a sport, craft, or art. So a congregation, especially in its life of worship, "traditions" people, involves them in something larger than themselves, something that is alive and creates a new world.

Crucial to acquiring skills, language, and tradition is a *master teacher* or *teachers*. For students of karate it is their *sensei,* who is honored with a bow whenever a student enters or leaves the school. Baseball has its coaches, oil painting or dance its master teachers. To learn any of these forms one must accept the guidance of a teacher. In some other endeavors we use a somewhat softer term, "role model" or "mentor," but the idea is the same: a person who loves and practices the art or sport. In the church's worship there are designated master teachers — the ministers and music directors — but there are also a host of other teachers, mentors, and role models who can help a person to learn what it means to be in the presence of God, to worship this God, and to live a life in which the God revealed in Jesus Christ is our center. The saints of the church are our *sensei,* our teachers. They are found in every congregation.

Finally, in learning a craft, art, or sport there is a *community* of present and past practitioners, persons who share a devotion to the endeavor and some broad notion of what constitutes excellence in it. For the painter it may be a school of painters or art critics. In karate it may be the *dojo* gathered to watch the match of beginning and more advanced students. Such communities provide support through their appreciation and recognition of accomplishment. They also provide accountability by rendering judgment as to who has attained a degree of excellence in the practice.

When one of us began attending church services again after

87

some years of absence from the church, it was at a small, urban, multiracial church that had roots in the African-American community. Looking back on that experience, which was a wonderfully formative one, he can see that each of these five elements was present. He was learning a certain set of skills — how to read the Bible, how to participate in liturgy, how to bear witness in weekly visits to a city jail as part of the congregation's outreach ministry. He heard a language, the language of Christian faith, both in the context of worship and in conversation. The language of faith was used meaningfully and authentically. There was a larger history or tradition, both a denominational one and that of the wider Christian church. There were master teachers, the pastor and church musician, but others as well, people with names like Rosie, Green, Maxie, Shirley, and Ernie. These master teachers knew much about what it is to live a Christian life, and they also knew how much they did not know, how much they still had to learn. And the congregation was crucial. There was a life and feeling to it, a presence that shaped him. Finding such a congregation, one longs to be part of it. The congregation itself has a personality that impacts those who sojourn there. This congregation and the two years spent in it began to form him as a Christian.

There is, we should add, something else required for formation to take place. There must be a receptive person, a seeker, a person whose heart and soul are at least somewhat open to God and to the formative work of a congregation. You have to want to play the game of baseball to get good at it. You have to love writing and language to become a writer. So, too, with Christian formation. Grace is at work, but part of grace's work is to create in us a longing, a restlessness for God.

In this new era the church must do both, both teaching and formation. Today, in congregations served by two of us, a new ministry attempts to join Christian formation and the teaching ministry of the church in a holistic way. Both congregations offer "covenant groups," groups of ten to twelve persons who have covenanted to be together in a special way over the next two years. Participants have committed themselves to take part regularly in the congregation's worship life, to attend core curriculum classes together, and to serve together in a social ministry of the church. In addition, participants in a covenant group meet together monthly to reflect on these experiences, on how God is present in the lives of members of the group, and so to contribute to each other's formation as Christians. Christian formation and the teaching ministry are two parts of the same whole. Jesus put these two parts together when he commissioned his disciples to go into all the world and make disciples, *baptizing* and *teaching* in his name. The two go together, baptism (formation in community) and teaching. That charge and that commission still stand!

Mission and Social Action: Beyond Common Sense

During the late sixties, in one of our home churches, a member of the governing board put forth a resolution that the church sell its building and give the proceeds to social service agencies in the inner city and organizations that advocate for justice in Washington. In speaking for the resolution the presenter said something like this: "It seems to me that, in times such as these, we have two clear choices: we can continue to worship here in this beautiful building — which benefits only us — or we can do something truly significant for others in this hurting world." The motion sent shock waves through that congregation, but there was a way in which the motion spoke to many, even to those who helped defeat it. How we spend our money is never a trifling matter, and when you worship the God who has a special concern for the poor in a large and ornate building, questions about how the church spends money cannot help but hit home.

What is striking today, however, is the presenter's assumption, found in varying degrees on both sides of the debate, that worship is for the benefit of those who gather to worship. Also, at a time when many people were engaged in monumental struggles with poverty, racism, and war, it was assumed that the only way for the church to make any positive contribution would be for it to divest itself of anything churchly and support those organizations that actually could make a difference.

One defining characteristic of the churches that formed us was the assumption that the church's primary mission is to help trans-form the world through political action. If you wanted to be, in a phrase of the times, "where the action is," you had to leave the church and go to the streets. The job of the church was to plead the cause of the poor and the oppressed before the thrones of power, to implore the powers of the age to be more compassionate and more just. The practices of the church were judged by whether they were "relevant" to this task in what was called "the real world."

In those days worship was deemed "political" only in the sense that it was in worship that you got your marching orders. That was where you heard a critique of the culture and were told how we were to go about changing the culture through political action. The ene-mies were named — most notably, poverty, racism, and war — but generally they were described as the enemies of every thinking, com-passionate person. For the most part, we stood for whatever socially concerned Americans stood for. It was in church, however, that we were given our religious reasons for hating the enemies we already hated and for believing in those things we already believed in. In those days, the means commended to Christians for addressing the hurts and injustices of the world were not notably different from those that were generally available to all people.

Those of us who took part in "politically active" churches took pains to distinguish ourselves from those who were only interested in "saving souls." We talked with disdain about those churches that were concerned with "getting its members into heaven." Neverthe-less, the distinction we wanted to make was never quite as clear as that. Even in our active liberal congregations we remember a lot of sermons about how to make our individual lives more bearable and fulfilling. The same preacher who one week told us that we could (and should) write our representatives in Congress on some particu-lar issue might the next week promise to show us how we could be free from anxiety and meaninglessness. In short, we were shown how we could make heaven on earth and save ourselves in the meantime.

We have come to see that, although the political and pietistic impulses of the liberal church seemed at the time to pull in very dif-ferent directions, they actually derived from the same sources. The emphasis was placed on what we could do to transform ourselves or society, and there was little mention of what God has done. Put another way, there was much diagnosis and prescription and little proclamation. The language that was used was largely borrowed from the social sciences. When the church addressed conventionally political issues it used the language of sociology, and when it addressed issues of personal piety it used the language of psychotherapy.

The result was a critique of culture that was not distinctive or even very deep. Generally, what the church offered by way of critique was already available elsewhere. Even when the church attempted to be "prophetic," often it did little more than echo back to the culture a religious form of the common wisdom. Is it any wonder, then, that there were those who wondered aloud if the church was really necessary?

It is important to stress that we still sympathize with many of the goals of the liberal churches that formed us. The economic injustices in our culture were, and continue to be, an abomination. Racism is a continuing scourge that needed, and still needs, to be addressed. The Vietnam War was an atrocity in ways that we did not fully appreciate even when we protested against it.

So it is not that the goals were unworthy, but simply that our efforts often had such shallow spiritual roots that it is not surprising that they have now withered. Many of the "radicals" of the sixties became the investment bankers of the eighties. Many of those who protested the Vietnam War were among those who cheered on the "smart bombs" of the Gulf War. Once some of the legislative gains of the Civil Rights movement were made, it lost steam. Most of the social service agencies that would have benefited from the sale of that church have long since shut their doors.

Today we have not lost interest in ministering to the hurting world, and we have not concluded that the church has no political role to play; but we understand that role differently now.

Stanley Hauerwas got our attention when he said, with characteristic bluntness, that the primary political role of the church is to be the church. This is what was forgotten in the political activism of the liberal church. All too often the liberal church assumed that the way for it to be political was to pass resolutions and make pronouncements. At the same time, the liberal church assumed that if we paid attention to the life of the community of faith, particularly its worship, that could only be understood as an attempt to escape from the world's problems. We now see that perhaps the most important thing we can do for the world, the most politically significant act we can make, is to gather to worship the Christian God in the midst of a culture that worships other gods.

Hauerwas's assertion that the primary political role of the church is to be the church has been criticized as an invitation to complacency. We have concluded, however, that such criticism derives from an inability to envision the far-reaching implications of such an image. To be sure, if the church exists only to make the lives of its members more bearable, or if we can conceive of politics only in very conventional ways, then the image will be inadequate. If the church were nothing more than the prayer chapel of the empire, then we would be right to reject the notion. But when we understand that the church gathers as the original counterculture that refuses to grant authority to the principalities and powers of the host culture, then we can begin to see what an ambitious and powerful image it really is.

The very existence of a community that worships God is itself a form of social witness. Governments have long understood this, and they typically respond to this threat either by attempting to domesticate the church (as surely has been the case in our culture) or by trying to wipe it out. After all, those who have erected altars to individualism, nationalism, consumerism, or any of the other -isms that demand our allegiance cannot long bear the existence of a living, visible, alternative community of faith that worships and responds to the claims of a different God.

During the year that West and East Germany were unified, one of our families hosted a young woman from West Germany. On the day unification was realized, she was particularly interested to learn whether the German churches rang their steeple bells. It seems that before she left home her own congregation was embroiled in a debate about whether it would be appropriate for them to toll their bells on that occasion. Those who were against tolling the bells argued that, as Christians, they had little at stake in a reconfiguration of the political landscape. They affirmed that, through baptism, they were already part of a worldwide fellowship that is not dependent on political recognition. As Christians our primary citizenship is not in any country but in the kingdom of God. They also recognized the need to view the actions of nation states with a vigilant skepticism, because the church is always in danger of being co-opted by the state.

Contemporary Germans may be particularly sensitive to this possibility. After all, the Nazis paid lip-service to the church because it was expedient to do so. With few exceptions, the church lost its independence. The church was domesticated by the state to such an extent that it lost its ability to speak out against the mounting atrocities that were occurring in German society. It may seem harmless enough to ring the church bells now, but it is important to assert the church's independence at such times so that it will be maintained in darker times.

We see something similar at stake in debates about whether the American flag has a place in the sanctuary of a Christian church. Similar battle lines are drawn when Memorial Day and Pentecost fall on the same weekend. On such a day a congregation faces a crucial choice: Are we to honor those who were sacrificed in their nation's wars, or are we to worship the God who united people of all nationalities in the community called church? In those times when the church refuses to honor national interests it becomes clear that worship itself can be a highly charged political act.

Admittedly, this requires an understanding of worship that is quite different from common assumptions. Once it was assumed that nothing the church does is more private than its worship. Worship was often seen as the gathering of individuals engaged in their own private communion with their God. But we have come to recognize that worship is a public and, therefore, political act. In worship we gather apart from the world, not to forget the world, but as a witness to the world and in order better to serve the world. So, again, sometimes the most effective thing the church can do for the world is to be the church.

Our encounter with God through worship is not simply a matter of getting our marching orders, so that we might leave knowing how we are to meet the needs of the world. If that were all that were required, then worship would be a simple matter. If we already knew what needs to be done, and we already had the character or strength or whatever else it takes to do it, then worship could be as simple and expeditious as a briefing session. If all we needed was to be informed, then such an approach to worship would be sufficient. If, however, those in need have a special claim on those who have encountered God, if the virtues required to address human need are cultivated in the community of faith, if more than being *informed* we need to be *formed* into faithful people for the sake of the world, then we will tend carefully to our worship. We can be informed quickly, but to be formed takes much longer. For such formation to take place, we will have to hear the scriptural story continually, pray countless prayers, and sing the same songs of praise over and over again.

One of us remembers worshiping with a large and active African-American church in the south side of Chicago that is known for its extensive outreach ministries. The order of worship seemed as thick as the Sunday *New York Times,* stuffed with pages that described opportunities for people to become involved in ministries to the community.

What was surprising, however, is that the worship service itself did not seem to reflect these same concerns. The sermon included no calls to action. Instead, the worship was filled with rousing gospel songs and resounded with the praise of Jesus. In fact, except for the prayers of intercession that were offered, there was no indication in the worship itself that the church is as involved as it is in community outreach. So, after worship, our colleague asked the pastor of the church, "Do you ever use the worship service to talk about mission?"

"Mission?" the pastor replied. "No, we *do* that. You white folk don't always seem to get this: Mission is not something you talk about; it's something you do."

Sensing that the visiting minister was a bit taken aback by his response, the pastor continued, "Look, the members of this congregation spend their whole week being told that they are nobody. Racism is worse than ever because the society pretends it's been conquered. More and more are trapped in a cycle of poverty. Should I tell them that they are supposed to go out and solve those problems? They are told all week that they are nobody.

"No, I've got two hours on Sunday morning to tell them that it's a lie. What they have heard all week is a lie. That's not easy. It takes a lot of singing. It takes a lot of preaching. I tell them, 'To God, you are somebody. You are precious. Christ died for you. He won't let you go. He won't forget you. You are a child of God.'

"Now, if after all the preaching and all the singing that truth really sticks to their hearts, it makes a difference. They leave changed. And if that happens, they don't need to be told that we can make a difference in the world. Christ died for you. That's what I tell them. But Christ died for others, too. Can you really believe something like that and not get involved in meeting the needs of all people? I don't think so. If we get the gospel straight, the rest will follow."

What this pastor said is not only true in the south side of Chicago. It is also true in Durham, North Carolina, or Seattle, Washington. The world gives us a lot of messages all week long about the way the world is ordered and our part in it, what deserves our allegiance and whom we should serve. We gather in worship to be reminded that there is another story, a decidedly different story, that gives us life.

It takes a lot of singing and a lot of preaching for us just to get the story straight. But, if after all the singing and all the preaching, that story nestles someplace deep, it makes a difference. We will leave worship changed. We will leave equipped to be witnesses to the risen Christ, not just in our worship, but in the world as well.

In our congregations we are beginning to recognize again the political significance of other common Christian practices. There was a time when the host culture provided at least tacit support for Christian practices; but now that the world is largely going its own way, the political significance of such practices is becoming clearer. For instance, when the culture at large tipped its hat to Christian practice by keeping stores closed on Sundays, the political significance of keeping the Sabbath was muted. Today, however, when the wheels of commerce grind continually through the week, it is again becoming clear that keeping the Sabbath is a political act.

After one of us spoke to his congregation about the role of keeping the Sabbath in Christian tradition, a couple in his congregation decided that they would take a step toward adopting this practice by not making purchases on Sundays. One Sunday the couple was in a department store looking at strollers for their new baby. They found one they liked and told the clerk that they would be back first thing on Monday to purchase it. When the clerk expressed surprise that they would want to wait, the couple explained that they were Christians who were trying to keep the Sabbath. The clerk responded, "I've never heard of anything like that before. That's . . . uh . . . interesting."

The clerk's response is not surprising. In a culture such as ours, where getting and spending have been elevated to civic duties, curbing our desire to acquire, even for a day, is a political act, subversive of the principalities and powers that demand our allegiance. It is telling, we think, that the practice of keeping the Sabbath took root among the Hebrews during a time of exile. When the Hebrews refused to work for a day it was a tangible reminder that for a time they may be under the power of their political enemies, but that power is limited. Their ultimate allegiance was to the sovereign God who rules over all.

Recognizing that we live in a time of exile is not an invitation to fold in on ourselves in self-concern. We view the church in this era as a mission outpost. If anything, we sense in our congregations an increased commitment to serving God's people in need, but today that commitment is expressed in different ways. In other times our concern for the hurting and hungry of the world was real enough, but often it was expressed in ways that kept us at a distance from those in need. We would send missionaries to a foreign land and receive dispatches about how they were serving on our behalf, or we would give money to social service agencies and church organizations that provided direct assistance.

Today there seem to be more and more Christians who want to be directly involved in what are sometimes called "hands-on" mission outreach efforts. Increasingly, our congregations offer opportunities to serve meals at local shelters, to build homes with the poor through Habitat for Humanity, to establish relationships with those who have mental retardation, or to bring meals to those who suffer from AIDS and are homebound. Our congregations also send groups to distant places to assist in health clinics, to dig septic systems, or to lay the foundation for a new church. We have learned from our colleagues around the country that great energy and commitment is flowing toward such ministries in an increasing number of congregations. Indeed, such ministries represent a fundamental shift in how we view our mission in the world.

There are those who complain that this new emphasis on "hands-on" mission outreach ministries derives from our need to feel good about our efforts. But we see it differently. Where once we served the poor, the sick, and the vulnerable because they need us, now we more fully recognize that we need them. Where once there would have been almost exclusive emphasis on how much we have to give, now we also freely and joyously recognize how much we stand to receive.

We are beginning to recognize what our Scriptures have long taught us: God has blessed the poor, the sick, and the vulnerable, so we want and need to be near them. We have much to gain and to learn from being with those God holds especially dear. So, we approach our mission efforts less as a beneficent gesture from those who have much toward those who have little. Instead, we see such encounters as more like an exchange of gifts, person-to-person, heart-to-heart. We often hear people say things like, "I signed up to help serve meals at the shelter because I wanted to give something back. But in just sitting down and talking with the folks and getting to know them over a period of weeks, I have gotten so much more in return." Although such statements are often made rather apologetically, we have come to see them as testimony to the ways we engage in such ministries and enter into such relationships in order to be transformed. We are not always the givers. We are also receivers. We have even come to recognize that, in God's economy, it is hard to determine who is the giver and who is the receiver because both participate in the endless echo of grace.

So we have learned to be quite up-front about the needs that we bring to our encounters with those whom God has particularly blessed. In one of our congregations a brochure describing an annual service project to Guatemala acknowledges this: "Two weeks may not be long enough to change Guatemala, but it is long enough to change your life forever."

Another of our congregations recently established a residence in the community for adults with mental retardation. The congregation bought a house to be used for this purpose and committed to being a supportive community for the residents. During a meeting in which this proposed outreach ministry was discussed, a member of the congregation asked how many people would benefit from what will be an expensive undertaking. Another member of the congregation replied, "Hundreds."

The questioner was obviously confused by the response: "Hundreds? I thought you said there would be only four residents."

The man then explained his answer: "Well, the way I figure it, there are the four residents, and their families and friends. Then too, the rest of us, who sometimes seem to prize competence and intellect above all, will benefit greatly from relationships with those who manifest the kind of acceptance, love, and other gifts of the Spirit that are not dependent on competence and intellect. I believe that this ministry has the potential of transforming not only the lives of the four residents, but also our church community and each of us as individuals. That's why I say that hundreds of us will benefit."

We are hearing more of these kinds of exchanges in our congregations as we claim the transformative power of being in relationship with those whom our God has called blessed.

We undertake such ministries, not as part of some grand social strategy, because increasingly we recognize that it is not our world to run. Instead, we see such outreach efforts as our opportunity to act out what we believe has happened in the world in Jesus Christ. It is not up to us to usher in the kingdom of God. Nevertheless, we can offer, through our relationships with those we aim to serve and find ourselves served by, a foretaste of that promised kingdom. So we care for those whom Jesus called blessed, the same ones the world considers a burden, as a witness to the world. Sometimes the world may deem our expressions of care as too small to be of consequence, but we also remember that Jesus said that the kingdom of God starts as something as small as a mustard seed.

We affirm that there are times when our encounter with God in worship and our encounter with human need in the world will lead us to involvement in more conventional political activities. That is, there are times when the church will approach the seats of power to plead the cause of those in particular need on behalf of the God who demonstrates special care for the least, the last, and the lost. Such advocacy can take many familiar forms that are commonly employed by those who want to affect the political process.

During the Constantinian Era that is just now passing, it was assumed that such advocacy was a rather simple matter. After all, the church operated on the assumption that it shared a common story, vision, and task with the civic leadership. Therefore, the church could make its appeals on the basis of what was assumed to be common sense.

Walter Brueggemann has made a helpful comparison with the era of the great prophets of Israel. He points out that the career of the prophets lasted only during the monarchy — that is, during a time when established powers were in principle committed to the same conversation as those who would appeal to them. There may have been a time in our nation's history when those who set out to be "prophetic" could operate under similar assumptions, but that time has now passed. When Christians approach the seats of political power today they cannot assume that they share with those in power a common understanding of the world. As Christians we see things differently because we stand in a different place, within a peculiar story that earthly powers do not recognize.

So, as appropriate as the church's involvement in public advocacy can be, there is an accompanying danger. Christians do not care for the world because of some universal impulse to do the right thing, but rather in response to the unique story of God's care for the world in the life, death, and resurrection of Jesus. The meaning and authority of this story are not recognized in the public sphere, filled as it is with people who do not see this story as their own. That is to say, much of the time we cannot expect others to know what concerns us, what motivates us, or even what we are talking about!

In an attempt to speak to the world, then, Christians have often translated their concerns into terms that might make sense to the world at large. There may not be anything necessarily wrong with translating the peculiarly Christian story into terms that can be more generally understood in the host culture. After all, often politics is a matter of finding common ground and building coalitions. Nevertheless, there is a danger that, in the search for common ground, the uniqueness of the Christian witness will be lost entirely. The church can come to represent just another lobbying group making the same arguments that could be heard elsewhere. Denominational gatherings can begin to resemble political conventions, the more liberal denominations talking like Democrats with a slight religious accent, the more conservative denominations saying little that could not be heard at a Republican party rally.

There is a further risk that, in attempting to speak the language of the surrounding culture, we might forget our native tongue. This is a particular danger in an era that might be thought of as a time of exile. In addressing a culture that does not share the Christian story, we can neglect or even forget the unique dimensions of that story. By approaching a political issue only in terms that others can readily understand, Christians lose the ability to make a unique contribution.

Recently one of us was a delegate to General Synod, the biannual national meeting of the United Church of Christ. One morning the General Synod paid extended attention to racial and cultural differences in an effort to further realize a commitment made at a previous Synod to become a "multiracial, multicultural church." San Francisco therapist and documentary filmmaker Lee Mun Wah discussed race and racism, and then the Synod viewed his film *The*

Color of Fear, which itself is a discussion among people of different races and cultures about race in America today.

Although the exercise had value, it also signaled the deeper problem facing the United Church of Christ and similar denominations. Issues of race and culture were approached through the lens and in the language of contemporary secular culture. That language, mostly psychotherapeutic, and not the language of the New Testament, set the terms of the discussion. There was no suggestion that the church, in struggling to be multiracial and multicultural, might find guidance as well as challenge in the book of Acts or Paul's letters to the Romans or the Galatians. In addressing these important matters, this gathering of Christians seemed unable or unwilling to speak in their own distinctive language or to be motivated by the peculiar faith they claim. On such occasions theology, once called the "queen of the sciences," can act like the kid sister who is flattered just to be allowed a small part in the conversation. No wonder no one seems to be listening!

Our story, rightly told, reflects different concerns than does the host culture. We think it is telling that African-American congregations seldom lose sight of this. In our society, African-American Christians have never had to fight off the illusion that they are in charge. Caesar was never a member of one of their congregations. For the most part, therefore, it has been clearer to African-American Christians that to speak the language of the host culture is to adopt the language of the oppressor. The history of African Americans in our nation is such that they are better prepared to recognize that their true power comes from another source, from the Christian gospel. So, even while addressing social issues in the surrounding culture, African-American Christians often speak in a way that is steeped in biblical imagery. We are not simply "citizens." We are "brothers and sisters" or "neighbors." Racism is not merely "unjust"; it is "sin." What we have to offer in response are not "social strategies" but "gospel."

Before Paul Sherry became president of the United Church of Christ he was executive director of the Chicago Renewal Society, a social service agency that has Christian roots. On one occasion he was invited to speak at the dedication of a new youth center. Another of the speakers was Harold Washington, then mayor of Chicago, who had many associations with Sherry. After the ceremony Sherry was surprised when the mayor invited him for a cup of coffee at a local diner. When they sat down Washington quickly got to the reason for his invitation: "You know, Paul, I appreciate all of your efforts in getting this center opened, and I also appreciated your remarks today. But you are a Christian minister and I didn't hear you say anything today that couldn't have been said by somebody else. We need to hear something else from you. We need to hear something from the gospel!" We do not think it is coincidence that this reminder came from an African American to a European American. African-American Christians have had more ample reminders that the language of the oppressive host culture is not enough to sustain social action. Something else is required, that something called gospel.

In addressing a culture that does not share the Christian story, we can neglect or even forget the unique dimensions of that story. Consider the debate concerning nuclear weapons that raged in our churches in the past decade. There were, of course, two opposing views. On one side of the debate were those who held that nuclear weapons are bad and should be abolished because they threaten the survival of civilization. On the other side were those who held that, although nuclear weapons are bad, they are necessary as a deterrent to ensure the survival of our way of life. Notice that, as heated as the debate became, both sides agreed that the fundamental issue — the greatest good — is our survival. But certainly one does not need to be a Christian to be in favor of survival. By approaching the issue in terms that others could readily understand, Christians lost the ability to make a unique contribution to the debate.

Our story, rightly told, has a distinctiveness that refuses to be accommodated. The Christian story seems strange to the world; and, because in part we are people of the world ourselves, there are times when it seems strange to us. It is a story filled with heroes and martyrs, foremost among them the one who died on Golgotha, for whom survival was definitely not the issue. In this story, the Romans were willing to put Jesus to death out of a concern for national survival. By contrast, our forebears in the faith were not ultimately concerned with the rise and fall of nations because they also saw themselves as citizens of another realm. They were willing to die rather than to kill because they viewed their own survival as less important than following the one who was willing to die rather than take up the instruments of violence. Needless to say, this is not a commonsense approach. But then, the world does not need the church to supply common sense; there are plenty of other sources. The church serves the world when it offers a decidedly uncommon perspective that is not otherwise available to the culture at large.

The abortion debate provides another telling example. Liberal churches, citing a "right to choose," square off against conservative churches, proclaiming a "right to life." In so doing, neither side adds anything to the public debate because both positions are already amply represented in the political arena. What is more, when we speak of rights we are speaking in a language that derives, not from our Scriptures, but from the Enlightenment philosophers. It is the language of the modern democratic state. The language of rights has so saturated the consciousness of those who live in the modern American culture that Christians within that host culture can sometimes forget that they have another way to talk about such matters that is quite different and distinctive. Our Scriptures do not speak of rights, but of duties, which are owed to God and to one's neighbor. Our story reminds us that life is not a right, but a gift. Life is a gift of God and belongs wholly to God, despite any appearances to the contrary. And when we receive gifts, obligations spread out in every direction. Notice that, if we bring this perspective to the issue of abortion, we can expect that there will still be differences of opinion; but the entire debate will be recast. Instead of echoing positions that are already well-worn in public debate, Christians would bring different and fresh questions to bear, questions such as: What are our obligations to the unborn? What are our obligations to mothers- and fathers-to-be who do not want or cannot care for children?

That is, when Christians enter the public arena, there will be times when we will act and speak in ways that are peculiar to the

Christian story. At such times we can expect that those who do not share that story will not understand us. It will seem to others as if we are speaking in a strange foreign language, and in a sense they will be right. We believe that the church can best serve the world, not by entering into important debates on the world's terms, but by speaking in peculiar ways that recast such debates in ways that reflect the distinctiveness of the gospel.

Nevertheless, because we are also citizens of the world, there may be other times when we can appropriately speak in ways that are more commonly understood. At such times we may appeal to commonly held standards of right and wrong. We may also join with others who do not share the Christian story if, in a particular instance, they are fighting the same evil we would fight or are pursuing the same good we would pursue. Even so, such alliances with fellow travelers will always be on an ad hoc basis. Inevitably, a time will come when we will have to travel our own way because our destination is the ultimate road less traveled, the one that leads to the cross and the empty tomb.

What the church has to offer the world is not commonsense approaches to the world's problems. What the church has to offer is something uncommon, something that is not otherwise found in the world we aim to serve, something that is both odd and peculiar — that something called gospel.

Conversion: New Creation

When John the Baptizer appeared on the banks of the Jordan, he encountered scoffers who resisted his invitation to enter the waters, to be baptized, washed, reborn. They perhaps doubted that the situation was so serious, that the measures needed were so drastic.

John the prophet warned them, "Don't say to yourselves, 'We have Abraham as our father, Sarah as our mother'" (see Matt. 3:9).

Don't take comfort in the past, in the old securities, in your conventional claims of privilege. God is able to raise up a people out of the stones in this river. This God is determined to have a family and will use almost any means to do it. Therein is our hope.

This book is a reflection by three pastors on the future of our church. As preachers, we stand up to speak each Sunday, and when we look out upon our congregations, what do we see?

— We see people who have lived through a time of loss, of relinquishment, North American Protestant Christians who have experienced our churches' most dramatic decline in history. Is our future one of continued decline?
— We see people whose perspective has been essentially the theology of accommodation, adjustment of the Christian faith to the cultural status quo with a corresponding loss of the distinctiveness and the peculiarity of the claims of Christ. If Jesus is simply one way among many, why bother to go there?

107

— We see people who have jettisoned the authority of Scripture, of church tradition, and of church discipline in favor of a radically subjectivized notion that truth is self-devised and self-validated. Is there anyone "out there" beyond the self who cares about us enough to guide and to sustain us?

And yet (and now for the Good News) we also see people who yearn for more. A time of loss, relinquishment, and disestablishment we name as exile might also be named as prelude to reconstruction and re-creation. Even amid relinquishment, God is doing a new thing. In exile, Israel showed a courageous determination to read her situation theologically. Israel kept asking, What is God up to in all this? What is God doing now?

Dismantling can be a prelude to rebirth. We in the Protestant mainline have been guilty of thinking that here, in North America, we had at last created a culture where it was safe to be a disciple of Jesus, where no one could get hurt being a Christian!

Furthermore, we had created a church, and a corresponding theology, that was so well accommodated to the reigning ideologies that conversion was no longer needed. Being Christian was roughly synonymous with being a caring, thinking human being. The Christian faith was reduced to common sense.

The Good News is that vast numbers of us in the mainline now know this to be untrue. In our relationships, in our families, in our own lives, we know something is wrong. The world feels chaotic, disconnected. Careening back and forth from disillusion with one after another promised path to fulfillment and salvation, we long for new lives but don't know where to begin. We have a hunch that what is wrong with us and our world demands more than some new technique for personal improvement, some new social program. We need a new world. We know we need more than improvement. We need re-creation.

The Good News is that this new world is breaking in among us, intruding into our settled arrangements, invading our consciousness. The future has a face, a name: Jesus. Here is a God who loves to create, who loves to raise the dead. Sometimes on Sunday, in worship, people receive a vision. They are given a new language whereby they are able to offer thicker descriptions of reality than otherwise would be available to them. They wake up to a new heaven and a new earth not of their own devising. In short, these exiles begin to move toward their true home. Christians name that homeward movement conversion.

A church member — talented, moving up in the world, an attorney — came to one of us in an attempt to make sense out of what had happened to her.

"Last Sunday, as the choir was singing at the end of the service, like it always does, I suddenly lost consciousness."

"Lost consciousness?" he asked.

"Like I fainted. But I didn't faint. It was like I stood there, with all the other people standing beside me, but I felt I was alone, bathed in the soft, warm, wonderful light. Then it was like I came back to myself. I looked around me and people were still standing there. I fell to my seat in the pew, deeply aware of having been embraced by something much greater than myself. It was wonderful. Like a door opened. Like God got to me."

"I wonder," he said, "if you lost consciousness or if you moved to a much deeper consciousness."

If this world and its present arrangements are as good as it gets, then conversion is not needed. Any basic change is looked upon as a threat by those who are satisfied with the present. People on top always protect their privileged perch. If your life is as eventful and adventuresome as can be expected, then conversion is not necessary. Relax, this is the best of all possible worlds.

In our pastoral experience, we meet fewer people who read the world or themselves in this self-satisfied way. We sense great yearning. One of the reasons why the Protestant mainline did so well during the 1950s was that we had wonderful theological justification for a time of cultural contentment and stability. One reason why our churches began to be troubled by the late 1960s and early 1970s was that our theology proved to be inadequate during a period when increasing numbers of Americans were saying, "There is something wrong." We had no way honestly to name the pain many were beginning to feel nor any real hope of extracting people from their unhappy present circumstances. We offered no promise of conversion — rebirth, new birth, forgiveness, salvation, detoxification, or any of the other ways the church has named conversion.

A recent stewardship campaign in one of our churches used the theme "Growing through Giving." The committee in charge of the campaign asked their pastor for some suitable scriptural verses on the theme of "growth" to use in their materials. When the pastor foraged through Scripture he discovered, somewhat to his surprise, that the theme of "growth" is not much in evidence in Scripture. Instead, the recurrent themes of Scripture are more startling: repentance, turning around, new creation. Perhaps the promised land of our longing cannot be reached through baby steps and gentle growth. Perhaps something more is required, something more like conversion. When the pastor's findings were shared with the committee, someone said, "It isn't difficult to talk about 'growth.' We do it all the time in other parts of our lives. Everyone wants to do a little better, including in our spiritual lives. From what you have shared, however, it sounds like we need 'new hearts.' But how do we tell the congregation *that?*" Indeed, we may not have told our congregations anything like that for some time.

We liberals have been guilty of presenting the Christian life as an orderly journey, a slow process of growth, "faith development." Sometimes it is. But Scripture also speaks of our relationship with Christ as a series of sudden lurches, of people being bumped, jerked, jostled by a God who will not abandon us to our own devices. Thus Annie Dillard says that we ought to hand people crash helmets rather than hymnals when they arrive for Sunday worship. With a living God, one never knows for sure where we may be by noon!

When we stand up to preach on Easter morning, we are used to seeing many unfamiliar faces, people who may not worship at any other time of year. It is tempting to begin with a disclaimer: "Before I begin, let me warn you that Easter is not a day for beginners. This is the advanced course, to be undertaken only after you have completed the introductory courses that deal with Jesus' life and teachings. Begin with the Sermon on the Mount. Marvel at Jesus' wisdom. Learn from him. If you begin there, perhaps you will be better prepared to hear this mysterious tale about Jesus rising from the dead." And yet, it is clear from the apostles of the early church and from the authors of Scripture that Easter is not the dramatic conclusion of the story for those who are able to follow it that far. Rather, Easter is the beginning. We do not need a few more helpful insights about our lives. We need new lives. A whole new world. Easter may be just the place for beginners, after all.

Conversion happens, real change is possible, not just because we feel a deep need for something better in our lives. Conversion occurs because God wills us not to be alone. Scripture shows that this God, the God of Israel and the church, keeps intruding, keeps revealing, keeps speaking to us. Our relationship to God is first of all something God does before it is anything we do. Call it Easter.

We confess that we have often been guilty of presenting faith as some innate human disposition, the highest and best of human aspirations. Years ago Freud and Feuerbach accused religious people of engaging in immature projection. We frail creatures need a God, so we project a God. What we call religion is dismissed as little more than collective human wish fulfillment.

"I've tried various therapies," she said, "even spent a month at a meditation center out West. Still nothing really worked for me. So now I'm trying church."

In a relentlessly therapeutic culture, we are not surprised that some think of Jesus and his church as just another means of getting what we want. Let's be honest. Sometimes the church has contributed unwittingly to the notion that Christianity is another helpful means to some good end.

"We are here in worship to get motivated to love and to serve others."

"I feel a sense of inner peace when I've been to church."

"The family that prays together stays together."

"Studies show that church attendance and good health go together."

Christians have historically claimed that we are in relationship to God in Jesus Christ because we have been called. God has graciously chosen us to be God's people. What we call "faith" is not some universal, innate human inclination toward some vague "divine." Faith is our relationship with the risen Christ. Faith is a name for our conversation with God in Jesus. To be in conversation implies speaking and listening between two distinct persons. Conversation implies a risk of being changed by the other with whom we are engaged. We speak to God in worship, in song, in prayer because we have been addressed by God. Our claim is that one cannot be in conversation with this self-revealing God without being changed.

"Every time I hear the story in one of your sermons," said one of our parishioners, "I turn just a little bit." That's not a bad description of the process of conversion to Christ. Daily we turn, finding our little lives drawn ever closer to God's intentions for us. We come to God looking for what we want, only to discover that we are being transformed into what God wants.

"It's like sometimes, in, say, listening to some passage of Scripture, or singing some familiar hymn, I wake up, my eyes open, and I say to myself, 'Right. This really is God's world and I'm part of it.'" That's not a bad way to speak of being born again. Our eyes blink; we see for real that which we had previously only professed; we believe. It's more than just a matter of coming to a new self-understanding. It's like immigrating to a whole new world. We wake up and are home.

Abraham left the familiar land called Ur because the Lord told him to set out for an unnamed land in which the Lord would dwell with him and his family. In his wanderings Abraham was sustained only by that promise and by his longing for a land in which he would build a home in the presence of God. The author of Hebrews wrote of Abraham and his family: "They confessed that they were strangers and foreigners on the earth, for people who speak in this way make it clear that they are seeking a homeland. If they had been thinking of the land they had left behind, they would have had opportunity to return. But as it is, they desire a better country, that is a heavenly one" (Heb. 11:13b-16a). This is not a desire for some heavenly home after we die, but rather for a home in which we are as much with God in this life as we might expect to be in the next. Once we are claimed by the promise of a home in the presence of God, a return to

112

the homes we left behind is no longer enough. Now we are drawn, not by a memory, but by a promise, and so our hearts are always marked by a certain longing.

We believe that our church must expend more effort helping people to name their present circumstances as exile, to relinquish their tight grip on the status quo, then to turn, to come home. We believe that this is not an impossible mission, for we are confident that God is already busy in the lives of late-twentieth-century Americans. The issue for our church is, will we be there joyfully participating in the movements of the Holy Spirit in our age, or will we mainliners sit on the sidelines?

As our friend Walter Brueggemann has said, "You preachers are world-makers. In your words, you make a new world. And if you won't let God use you to render a new world, then all you can do is to service the old one and that's no fun."

Preaching is one place we sense the difference. Although preaching is always a great challenge and hard labor, we find that we enjoy it, and even have fun, when we understand that our task is not to accommodate the faith to the present world or to make the gospel flow smoothly from what everyone already knows, but to point to and signal a new world.

It has been common in our experience and in our churches for people to be skeptical of preaching. Often preaching has been charged with being "outmoded" and "ineffective." Often people in the dominant culture have used the word "preach" only in a pejorative sense, as in, "Don't preach to me!"

Yet each of us has had the experience of preaching in predominately African-American congregations. There preaching is a communal act. There the congregation urges the preacher on to proclaim a truth and a word that the world does not know, which will not be heard elsewhere. "Preach it," call out members of the congregation. "Go on, say it," they urge, for they recognize that the preacher is called to say something daring, to give voice to a new creation, and that life depends in some strange way upon speaking and hearing this Word. Increasingly, we find people in our congregations yearning for such preaching, such a call to turn to be made new.

Rather than be content to keep house, running errands for the anxious affluent, soothing a bit of the pain for the nervous middle class, we ought to be pointing to and embodying a new world. Discipleship with Jesus ought to be fun.

A friend remembers attending two college reunions some fifteen years apart. At the first reunion, not long after graduation, he was enjoying his conversations with former classmates until they asked what he had been doing since graduation. When he responded that he was attending seminary, often they would nod politely and quickly change the subject. The response was not surprising. After all, in the minds of those who grew up in the sixties, the church was a partner in what was known as the establishment. Serving the church was viewed as about as interesting — and anti-establishment — as working for the IRS.

When our friend went back to another reunion fifteen years later, however, he noted a startling difference. His former classmates seemed eager to talk about his life and vocation, saying things like, "You're a minister, right? Tell me about that. I'm glad you weren't co-opted by the establishment. How did you come to choose such an unconventional path?" The contrast between these two experiences says less about how our friend's classmates had grown older and more about the ways in which the church is experiencing new life in our time. The church is much more interesting when it is disestablished.

How can we move from a maintenance mode of church life to a church that prays for, enjoys, and fosters conversion? We believe the future belongs to those congregations who develop the disciplines required for Christian resistance to the forces of a world that worships false gods. Exiles need to know that they are not home, that they live as strangers in a strange land. Then they need to cultivate those practices whereby they are enabled to survive as God's people in a land that doesn't know God. Daily disciplines like Bible study and prayer take on new significance as means of resistance.

A young adult told one of us, "I'm trying to use different words now."

"Such as?"

114

"Like rather than be so quick to describe my actions as a 'mistake,' now I try calling it 'sin.'"

Here is a young woman who is busy bending her life toward a countercultural path. She has learned that it makes all the difference which words we use. Think of Sunday worship as a struggle to answer the question, Who gets to name the world?

Don't call yourself "consumer," say "child of God."

Don't label someone as "male," or "heterosexual," say "brother."

Don't say, "I'm taking time off to do nothing," say, "I'm trying to keep Sabbath."

We, who have become so adept at describing our lives psychologically, economically, sociologically, must now work to describe ourselves theologically. It's like we have lost a language for having anything more interesting happen to us than a personal crisis. We have been so thoroughly schooled in atheistic descriptions of ourselves that, when God in Christ intrudes among us, we have no means to name revelation when we get it. Having lost a language of faith, we lack the resources and the imagination to think of life as anything more than chance, meaningless urges and counter-urges, one thing after another.

Therefore, crucial work for tomorrow's church is the nurture, the inculcation of our beloved language, our distinctive way of describing what is going on in the world. In exile, Israel invented the synagogue as sacred space whereby God's people gathered to tell the story, name the name, pass on the faith to their young. We expect that more of our churches will come to resemble the synagogue more closely.

Time and again, in reading Scripture, we are reminded of what is required to be in conversation with the God of Israel and the church. No pale, limp projection of ourselves, this God comes to us (Bethlehem), keeps resisting us, exposing us, unmasking us (Calvary), then, even after we have done our worst, keeps coming back to us (Emmaus). No one walks away from encounters with this living God unscathed. Conversion — radical, life-long turning from ourselves toward God — is a hallmark of conversation with the God named Trinity.

We have written this book as our pastoral attempt to tell what we have heard in our conversation with God in behalf of our congregations. We speak out of the joyful confidence that God is able to produce the sort of people whom the gospel deserves. Jesus Christ has given himself to and for the world, and he will not desist until he reigns, until the purposes of God are fully realized and Christ is all in all, for all.

The gracious promise is that God wants a people, a family. Churches can be born again no less than individuals. Exile, the silence of the wilderness, is a wonderful location better to hear the call toward home.